IAN BOTHAM

The great all-rounder

IAN BOTHAM

The great all-rounder

DUDLEY DOUST

CASSELL

LONDON

CASSELL LTD.

35 Red Lion Square, London WC1R 4SG
and at Sydney, Auckland, Toronto, Johannesburg,
an affiliate of
Macmillan Publishing Co., Inc.,
New York.

First edition May 1980
First edition, second impression June 1980

ISBN 0 304 30606 1

Printed and bound in Great Britain at
The Camelot Press Ltd, Southampton

To
KATHRYN and JANE

ACKNOWLEDGEMENTS

For help and advice in the preparation of this book, the author wishes to thank friends at *The Sunday Times*, many generous cricketers, the BBC and Norman Harris (for loan of videotapes), Wendy Wimbush and Bill Frindall (for checking the statistics), Enid Watson (for typing the manuscript) and, not least, a certain R. Millichip who found and turned in to the Metropolitan Police a lone, late version of the manuscript, found on the streets of London.

Photo Acknowledgements

Central Press Photos   40, 47
Daily Mirror   57
Daily Telegraph Colour Library   96, 109 bottom
Patrick Eagar   xiii, 7, 8, 12, 15, 18, 21, 25, 27, 31, 35, 47, 53, 55, 61, 64, 65, 71 top, 93, 105, 112, 113, 115, 117 top
Ken Kelly   xii, 51, 67, 86
Keystone   29
Adrian Murrell   4, 69, 71 bottom
Chris Smith   117 bottom
Sun photo by P. Jay   98

CONTENTS

FOREWORD

The first time I spoke at any length with Ian Botham was when I was preparing a profile of him for *The Sunday Times* in the summer of 1978. Ian was then 22 years old and well launched into his career: nearly five seasons as a Somerset regular, fifty-four weeks with England. His record was impressive and garlanded with fine photographs: Botham, the neophyte Somerset player, blooded into stardom by a crumpling ball from Andy Roberts; Botham, the batsman, savaging a ball with his own special fury; Botham, the bowler, dishevelled and soaking in sweat, his trousers hanging down round his hips, charging down the wicket with his arms flung high.

It was all stirring stuff but to me the photograph that opened and closed the shutter on the young England all-rounder was taken at the moment of running a man out that summer in a Test match at Lord's. It depicts Botham thundering towards us, all 15 stone of him, and at the last moment launching forward to shovel the ball into the stumps. It captures him perfectly: a cricketer, rapt in his game, and woe to the man who gets in his way.

That the victim of the run-out in this picture should have been Richard Hadlee of New Zealand is particularly piquant, given the rivalry between the men, but this is a different story and appears elsewhere in the book. What lingers round Patrick Eagar's splendid picture is the aura of Botham's aggression. It was this aggression, rather un-English, that interested me, when I visited Botham. What was it all about? He sat in his rented house in Weston-super-Mare, an enormous leg draped over the arm of a living-room chair, and tried to dig up the roots of this will to win.

He didn't like this sort of grilling, but he would give it a go. The aggression didn't spring from a deprived childhood or an early insult or, as far as he could tell, from any need to flatter his vanity. It was just *there*. He was attempting to explain this when, suddenly, the door crept open and his infant son, Liam, came crawling towards him across the carpet. Botham's leg thumped down on to the floor and he burst into laughter. 'Now, there is a good example of what I am talking about,' he said, opening his arms to the child, gathering him up with all the gentleness common to big men. 'If we're playing some silly game, Liam and I, I can't let him win. It's pathetic. I've even got to beat my one-year-old child.'

Botham was a brawny fawn that day, solicitous to his attractive little wife Kathryn as she prepared lunch, light on his training shoes as he walked round the house with his boxer bitch, Tigger, cradled in his arms. 'Brian Close has a boxer, as well,' he said, 'and

ix

when Tigger is older we're going to put her to him.' Somehow I tried to picture an amalgam of Close and Botham, rather than of the dogs, and then we went to lunch. Botham was in a gentle, shy mood and, as I recall, he wanted to know all he could about his hero, the Spanish golfer Severiano Ballesteros. Could he *meet* Ballesteros? Maybe one day they could play together in a pro-am tournament? Botham, despite his blustery exterior, is a modest man who prefers not to talk of himself.

The following summer, when we began work on this book, I visited the Bothams in another rented house in Weston. Something was wrong with the look of the place. Something terrible had happened to the kitchen door. A panel was caved in, the wood broken and splintered. Kathy gave a little smile. 'Ian,' she said, 'had a bad game at Taunton the other day and he came home and kicked in the door.' Indeed, Botham can be a man of dark tempers but, equally, the broken door stood as brutal testimony to Ian's commitment to cricket, whether with England or Somerset.

A third encounter with Ian came that summer at the Weston-super-Mare Golf Club. Brian Rose, the Somerset captain, and I, two left-handers, had challenged Botham, handicap 11, and his father to a better-ball match. The match see-sawed, Rose doing much of the sawing for us, and the match landed all-square on the eighteenth tee. The eighteenth at Weston is a par 5, with an out-of-bounds running down the right-hand length of the fairway. Rose and I played down the middle. Botham's father sliced a ball out-of-bounds. Ian, something of a slicer himself, set up safely, aiming about 45 degrees off towards the sea. He hooked a screamer, safe enough, but about two fairways off line. I mumbled to Rose that that was it, the match was ours. Rose smiled. He had played too much golf and cricket with Ian to agree. 'Mmmf,' he sniffed. 'Never count Both out – of anything.' And lo and behold, one more gigantically hooked wood, an outrageous chip and a 15-foot putt and Ian had won the hole and the match with a birdie 4.

Never count Botham out – of anything. Rose's warning can be addressed to Botham's Test opponents over the past few years for, at the risk of an ocean of contrary evidence, I will advance a dangerous claim: no man in cricket history has participated in a bigger percentage of his team's Test dismissals while on the field than Ian Botham of England. In his 25 Tests, from his debut against Australia in 1977 to the India Golden Jubilee Test in 1980, Botham's part in the fall of rival wickets reads like this: wickets 139, catches 36, run-outs 3, for a total of 178.

In that period, *and while Botham was on the field*, a total of 393 enemy wickets fell to England. By my reckoning, this means Botham had a hand in 45·29 per cent of the rival Test wickets that fell. Given the fact that no man has taken as many wickets in fewer tests, given the high level of modern close-fielding, it is hard to imagine anyone surpassing this record.

How good is Botham? As an American who first watched a full 3-day cricket match in 1977, when the Australians played Somerset at Bath, I claim no historical perspective whatever. Yet it was little more than two seasons later that cricket followers, more expert than I, began gingerly comparing him to three of history's great all-rounders: England's Wally Hammond, Australia's Keith Miller and, most exalted of all, Botham's own childhood hero, West Indies' Sir Garfield Sobers.

At the time of our first long meeting in the summer of 1978 Botham had played in only ten Tests. At this point in a book which will be heavily freighted with statistics, it is perhaps interesting to compare Ian's record with the other great all-rounders of the game.

Batting

	Tests	I	Runs	NO	HS	Avge.	100s	50s	Ct
Hammond	11	13	500	1	108	41.66	3	1	12
Miller	17	23	791	1	108	35.95	3	3	23
Sobers	21	28	1035	1	137	38.33	4	3	33
Botham	25	35	1336	2	137	40·48	6	3	36

Bowling

	Balls	Runs	Wkts	Avge.	BB	5W/I	10W/M
Hammond	2554	1059	64	16·54	8–34	8	1
Miller	3822	1626	87	18·68	8–34	8	1
Sobers	4896	2098	107	19·60	8–34	10	1
Botham	6228	2575	139	18·52	8–35	14	3

Based on these statistics, and those that keep coming in, Botham plainly has the makings of a great all-rounder and to those sceptics who, in a diminishing chorus, would claim he has not faced the quality players of old, I can say only two things. One, nostalgia is a blinding disease, rife among the English. Two, consider the case of Bobby Jones, the American golfer, who exactly a half a century ago won the Grand Slam, the Open and Amateur titles on both sides of the Atlantic. Jones beat the competition that was set before him, good and mediocre, throughout his short career, and what more could be asked of a sportsman?

Finally, a word on the structure of the book. It includes the story of Ian's life, from his birth in Cheshire, through his childhood and youth in Yeovil and into his married life in Epworth, South Humberside. It sketches in his career with Somerset, and with a broader brush deals with his career as an England Test player, including his 1979–80 tour of Australia and, best of all, his amazing performance in the India Jubilee Test in Bombay in February 1980, a dazzling display that never before has been seen in the game.

The book, however, is basically built round two major moments in Ian's cricket life, his 100th Test wicket and his 1,000th Test run, his record double, achieved during the India tour of England in 1979. In choosing this structure, I was lucky that Ian's leading adversaries in the drama were two eminent Indians, Sunil Gavaskar and Bishen Bedi, who were generous and perceptive in reliving the moments of their battles with Botham. I am lucky, too, and grateful, for such a patient and thoughtful subject as Ian Botham. He gave hours and hours of his time to the project.

Dudley Doust
West Bradley
Somerset
March 1980

Ian Botham: a cricketer, rapt in his game.

Triumph! The salute, when a wicket has fallen: another one for Botham.

ONE

August 2, 1979

Dull clouds, driven south through the night were littered over London. The clouds, according to a London Weather Centre forecast issued at 6 a.m., would increase during the morning. The afternoon would be mainly cloudy. Showers were expected later in the day and while they might be heavy and prolonged, the outlook for Friday was for a warmer day with sunny periods and only isolated showers. The temperature on the roof of the London Weather Centre was 15 degrees centigrade at 5 a.m.

Jim Fairbrother, the groundsman, had heard the recorded weather report as he put the kettle on in his little house opposite the nets at Lord's Cricket Ground. He was sceptical of the message and now he stood uneasily in the middle of the pitch. It was 7.30 on the morning of August 2, 1979. The Second Cornhill Test match between England and India was due to begin in four hours' time and Fairbrother was faced with a dilemma. Should he or should he not take the covers off the strip? It could rain at any moment. It would be daft to expose the wicket to a pelting rain. On the other hand, he told himself, the wicket belonged to him: it would until the umpires came on – and if he didn't get it mown and rolled before it *did* rain he wouldn't be doing his job.

Fairbrother glanced at the sky. A lone gull, wheeling overhead, suggested rough weather moving in from the sea. The gull cried out and dropped, strutting, into the outfield. Fairbrother recognised the bird and from this drew comfort. It was a herring gull, one of a family that nested on the roof of the grandstand, over near the Father Time weather vane, and its presence suggested nothing at all. Fairbrother took his decision. He called his staff of six and, together, they set about shifting the big green tarpaulin, revealing a golden wicket. On this wicket a young England cricketer was to bowl himself into history.

The young cricketer was Ian Botham, who at the time was 23 years and 251 days old. The record he sought was a bowling one. With 94 test wickets to his credit, he aimed to become the fastest man, in terms of time, to take his 100th Test wicket since the inaugural Test match between Australia and England in 1876. Indeed, there had been bowlers, four in all, who had reached their 100th wicket in fewer Tests, fewer innings, fewer balls. The medium-paced George Lohmann, of England and Surrey, led the list. He had turned the trick in 16 Tests, reaching his bowling century in a purple patch at Johannesburg in 1896, while dismissing nine batsmen with 72 balls in the first innings of a triumph over South Africa. A year earlier, Charles 'The Terror' Turner, an Australian of quick pace, used up all the 17 Tests he was to play in to achieve his 100th

1

wicket, all of them, it might be added, against England. The durable Syd Barnes of England, Warwickshire, Lancashire and Staffordshire also spent 17 Tests in reaching his 100th wicket. Barnes' first wicket was that of Victor Trumper at Sydney in 1901; and a level dozen more were to be taken off the great Trumper before Barnes reached his century wicket some eleven years later, again against Australia at Sydney. Clarence Grimmett, the Aussie with the devastating leg-breaks rounds off history's trio who (at least at this writing) reached their 100th wicket in 17 Tests. Grimmett took his amid a clatter of nine West Indian wickets at Brisbane in 1931. There also was a bowler, Graham McKenzie of Australia and Leicestershire, who was younger than Botham when he achieved his 100th Test wicket. The pacy McKenzie was 23 years and 163 days old when, in December of 1964, he took his 100th Test wicket in a match played against Pakistan at Melbourne.

Of all these records, Botham knew absolutely nothing. What he did know, however – and of this the Press had been making him restlessly aware throughout the summer – was that Andy Roberts, the fiery West Indian, had set him a target. Roberts held the record for the quickest time spent in collecting his 100th Test wicket: 2 years and 143 days. Students of cricket minutiae – Botham is not one – remember the circumstances surrounding that milestone wicket taken by the big fast Antiguan. So does his victim, David Steele, who was seen off by one quick bowler after another in his short Test career. The wicket fell on July 27, 1976. England were batting in the second innings against the West Indies at Headingley, chasing a lead of 259 runs which, ultimately, they failed to attain. 'I wasn't very pleased with the ball because I'm not sure I hit it,' later recalled Steele, who has gone prematurely grey in the service of the game. 'It pitched outside the off stick, I sparred away and heard nothing. The West Indians went up, the umpire said, "Yes, caught behind" and, thank you very much, Andy had his 100th Test wicket.'

At about the same time as the Lord's groundsman was rolling his strip, and some two miles to the south, Botham awoke to a knock on his door in the Charing Cross Hotel. It was the hall porter, bearing his morning tea and newspapers, the *Daily Telegraph* and, largely because he writes a ghosted column there, the *Sun*. Botham's rise from sleep is a struggle, full of stretches and yawns, and it was some time before he threw his legs over the edge of the bed. Sitting there, stark naked, rattling spoon after spoon of sugar into his tea cup, he looked more like a rugby prop forward than cricket's first modern superstar. He wore his sandy blond hair long and curly at the neck and thick in the moustache; this style, while currently fashionable, gave him the stern look of a Victorian father or, sterner still, the menacing aspect of a Mississippi riverboat gambler.

One's first impression of Botham is that his features are big. His nose is long, remarkably fine and pointed, but from bridge to tip, it wanders. It has been broken more times than he can remember: once while batting in the nets during the 1977–78 England tour of Pakistan and New Zealand, more recently while training with the Scunthorpe United football team during the close season. Botham's blue eyes, still small with sleep, are set wide apart under strong bony brows, the sort of brows which would cut easily if he were a prize fighter. One of his eyes, the right one, is larger and rounder than the other and this, according to the England team physiotherapist Bernard Thomas, is not uncommon among sportsmen. 'This could be the result of a weakened eye or a hearing defect, but I doubt it,' Thomas will say, 'I have found that people who grow up working very, very hard on a single-sided sport, such as a young cricketer looking down a wicket, sometimes develop in this unilateral way.'

Botham is 6 ft 2 ins tall and weighs nearly 15 stone; judging from the fact that he had gained more than a stone in the last year, he may still be growing. Surprisingly, his shoulders are narrow and sometimes, when he suffers a rare attack of 'exercise asthma' on the field, they look narrower still, for he will instinctively clamp his shoulders round his chest in the effort of breathing. However, what strikes you most about his physique are his thighs: absolute tree trunks, great oaken things that form the massive foundation for his power with the ball and the bat. Also, there is a tremble of fat round his tummy. It is there, all right: Thomas can and does snatch it up amply in the jaws of a calliper. Thomas rebukes Botham for plundering puddings from round the England dinner table. He would like to see his young bowler lose half a stone, principally to increase his mobility, improve his hip rotation and, perhaps most important, reduce the merciless pounding his feet take in bowling. It is not in Botham's nature to take, or at least to *appear* to take, such advice and after first flatly denying the excess fat he will defend it. 'I'm quite happy carrying the extra weight,' he will say. 'The way I see it, I've got to have some fat to draw on. As a matter of fact, maybe this is one of the reasons I can bowl for such very long spells.' Botham's justification of this fat, while a small issue, illustrates one of his maddening, mulish charms. His friend and team-mate at Somerset, Peter Roebuck, recognises this trait in the man. 'In an argument, if Ian gets on the defensive, you're in trouble,' Roebuck will explain, 'with his back to the wall, he will attack and construct a pretty solid rationale for his ideas.'

Botham's aggressive temperament has left him with an abundance of scars. They speak of a robust, almost reckless life. There is an ugly scar under his right bicep, which was closed by sixty stitches, the abiding evidence of a school holiday accident on Exmoor. A tree limb snapped under his weight and his arm was ripped as he fell past the jagged edges. He is neither squeamish nor titillated as he tells the story. 'There was blood going everywhere, which was funny because I didn't feel too bad. They carried me down the hill on a stretcher and I still didn't think I was hurt until they cut my shirt sleeve off. A woman passed out when they were loading me into the ambulance.'

Another childhood scar, a neat puncture wound on his right calf, was suffered one Christmas Eve in Yeovil, his hometown in Somerset. On that occasion Ian fell off his bicycle and a pedal plunged into his leg. Here again, the injury wasn't serious. 'I think that was the best Christmas I can remember,' he says, 'I was spoilt. I was continuously carried round from room to room.' There is also a ragged scar on his right thigh, the result of an untreated injury. 'It didn't heal too well because I couldn't tell anybody about it,' Botham relates. 'You see, I got into this punch-up in the schoolyard. I gave the guy a hiding but, in the process, I cut my leg on some barbed-wire.' As Botham speaks of these injuries you get the impression that he may be courageous but, above all, he is fearless. He agrees with this, especially when the judgement applies to sport. 'I don't think I've ever been scared in sport,' he will say; 'there is one thing I can't stand, and that is people who are afraid. The day I worry about being hurt in cricket is the day I'll pack in the game.'

One injury, nonetheless, was briefly worrying. It left a nasty scar across his left wrist – it lay there for months like a dead white worm – and its cause is sometimes unfairly interpreted. It happened in the Queen's Head, a pub near his home in Epworth, South Humberside, on the occasion of a going-away party two days before he left on the

Botham, ever the aggressor, even in practice. Like each of the England players, he has a special routine laid out by the team physiotherapist, Bernard Thomas; his being filled with stretching exercises to limber his huge muscles. Notice his massive torso, proportionately bigger than his legs. Notice, too, how he dwarfs England captain, Mike Brearley.

Wraps off. Botham, in Australia 1978–79, ready to resume cricket after his harrowing accident suffered before setting out from England.

England tour of Australia in 1978. He cut it on a glass door in the pub. He did not put his fist through the glass door in the act of taking a swing at somebody or some thing, and his proof of this sounds persuasive: 'If I was going to hit somebody, I'd hit him with my right fist.' In fact, cold sober and walking to the gent's, he had reached out for a door and put his hand accidentally through the glass pane. He severed two tendons and came within a hair's breadth of cutting a nerve. The fact that Botham, his wrist spurting blood, immediately flexed and unflexed his fist to test the extent of the injury, suggests the detached view many sportsmen take of their bodies. As far as pain mattered, the wound might just as well have been a cracked bat to Botham, or a stud come loose on his boot. The injury does not bear thinking about: if the nerve had been sliced, Ian would have been left with a claw-hand and no playing future in cricket.

The single flaw in his frame that conceivably could shorten his cricketing career, Botham feels, is his left ankle. The ligaments and joints there are weak. In his childhood, he 'turned over' the ankle several times in various games and, in the match in which England won the Ashes at Headingley in 1977, Botham fractured it when he

4

stepped on a ball. 'That ankle is something that might mess me about one day,' Botham will say, shrugging. 'But I can't bother worrying about it. If the ankle goes, it goes.'

The ankle is fine on the day of the Lord's Test and Botham got up feeling fit in his hotel room. He had begun to dress − crisp cords, the England blazer but no necktie since he feels and looks throttled in a tie − when a knock came at the door. The knock was fainter than the hall porter's had been and it came at about the height of the keyhole. It was his son, Liam. The child had come from the room across the hall, where Botham's wife and second child, five-month-old Sarah, were staying for the Test. Liam, nearly two years old, is blond and sturdy and moves with an aggressive shoulder-roll which, one can suppose, is his attempt to copy his father. He is devoted to his father and feels deprived of his company. Altogether, the boy probably has seen his travelling father only about five months of his life. Liam will happily watch his father play cricket on television but once, when he saw Ian being interviewed in his street clothes on the box, he burst into tears. It was all too much. If Daddy wasn't wearing white clothes, he sobbed, he ought to be at home.

Ian and Kathryn Botham are keenly aware of the sacrifices they and the children are making during Ian's pursuit of his career. This was made plain to them, in a gale of bluster, by Brian Close. Close has a special interest in the couple. He was Botham's captain and early mentor at Somerset, now sits in judgement of him as an England selector and yet is closer still to Kathryn. She is the daughter of Gerry and Jan Waller, old friends of Close, who live at Thorne, near Doncaster. In fact, Close stayed with the Wallers during the brouhaha that surrounded his sacking as captain of England in 1967 and it was during that time that he became a favourite 'uncle', protectively affectionate towards little Kathryn. Kathryn met Ian during Close's captaincy of Somerset and when he was told of their planned marriage, he blew into a bona fide rage. He got the news from Jan Waller because the youngsters were frightened to tell him. 'If Ian does anything to hurt Kathy, I'll *kill* him, and if Kathy stands in the way of Ian's career, I'll give her a roasting as never was.' Close cooled down sufficiently to attend the wedding in January of 1976 and to stand as a godfather of Sarah.

Liam stayed in Botham's room to watch him dress and shave. At the mirror, Ian combed his hair, carefully turning in the curls with a long, round hairbrush. He softly patted it all into place. The care he takes with his hair, while appearing out of character, is one of Ian Botham's few concessions to vanity. He was ready for his public who, doubtless, would be waiting outside the hotel and swarming round his car as he drew up to Lord's for that Second Test against India.

5

TWO

Roots of Aggression

Botham signs his autograph with a tight, muscular gesture, jerky and bulbous, and at the end of it, as though delighted to break free from constraint, he adds a full and artful lasso. The signature is nearly indecipherable. It took a trained graphologist, sliding an England team autograph sheet under a microscope, to determine that he has written 'Ian' and not his initials 'I.T.' before his surname, Botham.

The graphologist who examined Ian's signature was Joan Cambridge, a member of the Scientific Council of the European Society for Handwriting Psychology, who gives evidence in High Court. Overall, she found that Botham, unlike some players, stayed scrupulously within his allotted patch on the page. This suggested a respect for the rights of other people. As for the signature itself, it strove basically for balance. The lasso had a balanced forward and backward swing. The full, downward expansion of the capital 'B' provided a nice balance in a signature that lacked such downward-looping letters as 'g' or 'y' and was an example if Ian's dynamic use of space.

The graphologist, calling attention to Botham's variety of circular movements in his signature, together with the left-tending downstrokes to form them, suggested that the signature was contrived in his childhood. 'However, even when a signature is produced with a degree of artificiality,' Miss Cambridge went on, 'and in accordance with a person's desire as to how it should appear, it has significance as an indication of how the signatory sees himself.'

Botham's autograph indeed was contrived in his childhood and perhaps, too, as an indicator of how he wanted to see himself. Ian worked hard on his autograph as a boy. At about six, when other children were practising joining up letters in simple barnyard words, he would come home from Penmont School in Yeovil and practise joining up the letters of his name. His mother asked him why he did it so ceaselessly. 'I've got to practise it,' he would say. 'When I get older, people will want my autograph.'

Such boyish bumptiousness is not usually associated with Somerset lads and, in fact, Ian descends from North Country stock. The surname 'Botham' is thought by the family to derive from the Scots word 'bothy' or 'bothie' which is defined by *The Concise Oxford Dictionary* as a 'hut, cottage; one-roomed building in which workmen are lodged', perhaps a 'booth' in origin. As for the pronunciation of the surname, confusion abounds, even within the family. In Somerset, home county of Ian, the 'o' is short, as in 'pot'. In Yorkshire, home of his antecedents, the 'o' is long, as in 'boat'. Although Ian is happy enough with either pronunciation, he prefers the North Country

ENGLAND TOUR TO AUSTRALIA AND INDIA
1979-80

Captain - J. M. BREARLEY (Middlesex)

Vice Captain - R. G. D. WILLIS (Warwickshire)

D. L. BAIRSTOW (Yorkshire)

I. T. BOTHAM (Somerset)

G. BOYCOTT (Yorkshire)

G. R. DILLEY (Kent)

G. A. GOOCH (Essex)

D. I. GOWER (Leicestershire)

M. HENDRICK (Derbyshire)

W. LARKINS (Northamptonshire)

J. K. LEVER (Essex)

G. MILLER (Derbyshire)

D. W. RANDALL (Nottinghamshire)

R. W. TAYLOR (Derbyshire)

D. L. UNDERWOOD (Kent)

P. WILLEY (Northamptonshire)

Manager - A. V. BEDSER

Asst. Manager - K. F. BARRINGTON

Physiotherapist - B. W. THOMAS

Scorer - G. G. A. SAULEZ

The England team autograph sheet. Hundreds are signed, a graphologist's dream. Note that Mike Hendrick, returned to England injured, is replaced by Yorkshire's Graham Stevenson and that Geoff Miller, dropped, is replaced by Middlesex's John Emburey.

Ian, nicknamed Guy the Gorilla, at a Christmas party during the 1978–79 tour of Australia.

'Bow-tham'. His nicknames? 'Both', with the short 'o'. Or 'Guy the Gorilla', after the popular inmate of London Zoo.

Ian's most famous forebear, whatever he was called, certainly did not live in a bothy or hut or booth. He was grander than that. John Cherry, a great-great-grandfather and kin to an early Botham, was a Yorkshire inventor who developed a centrifugal pump which was much used in the building of the Panama Canal. Ian's paternal great-grandfather, a man from York, was a patternmaker, as was his son, who later moved to Hull and went into ship-fitting. It was there that Ian's father, Leslie, was born. Leslie was a useful all-round sportsman as a child and, upon leaving high school, just before the war, joined the Fleet Air Arm. Chief Petty Officer Botham, a naval aircraft apprentice, went on to play at a high level in soccer, cricket and hockey during his career in the Navy.

Ian's maternal antecedents trace back to Cumberland where a great-great-grandfather, a mid-Victorian sea captain named Henderson, put out from Whitehaven in the schooner *Huntress*. A great-grandfather, Joseph Higgins, sort of a seaman as

8

well, was Harbour Master at Maryport and, according to a newspaper cutting of 1892 which depicts him pondering a chess move, chess champion of Cumberland. Higgins also was a water diviner and Ian's mother remembers her old grandfather walking over her father's Cumberland farm, a twig held in his hand. Her father, Albert Collett, died before she was born and in her early girlhood young Marie Collett moved with her kinfolk to Bradford. She grew up in Yorkshire, playing badminton, hockey and cricket, and trained as a general nurse. In the War, she served as a Voluntary Aid Detachment dental nurse.

Les and Marie met at HMS *Ariel*, in Lancashire, and married in Scotland. Their first child, Ian Terence, was born on November 24, 1955, in Heswall, Cheshire, where the Bothams kept a home while Les was stationed at the Fleet Air Arm near Londonderry in Northern Ireland. In honour of Scotland they intended to name him 'Iain', in the Scots manner but, flustered, Les mistakenly registered him Ian. Ian moved straight away to Northern Ireland, where, at the age of two, he emerged as an uncompromising competitor. 'We had organised a foot race, maybe 20 yards, among Navy children,' his mother recalls. 'Ian wasn't much of a sprinter in those days – in fact he never *was* much of a sprinter – but this time he got out in front and near the finish line he turned suddenly and bumped down the other children, one by one, and finished the race by himself.' A year later, Les Botham retired from the Navy and the family moved to Yeovil where he had taken an appointment as type-test engineer at Westland Helicopters Ltd. 'Ian's favourite pastime once we got to Yeovil,' his mother continues, 'was to throw a hammer through the lounge window.'

Ian's rampant behaviour as a little boy was tempered by a will to learn. When he wasn't chucking the hammer around the house, he was wandering off and climbing through the hedge surrounding the nearby Yeovil Boys' Grammar School. There he would fetch balls or stand quietly studying the boys at play. 'One day I was in the kitchen and Ian, who was then about four, came in with a cricket ball,' his mother recalls. 'He looked at me and looked at the ball. And then said, very seriously, "Do you know how to hold a ball when you're going to bowl a daisy-cutter?" He showed me the grip and then disappeared to practise his daisy-cutters.' He was growing accustomed to playing sport with his elders as well, for on week-ends he would tag along, his kit tucked into the back of the family car, as his father went to play cricket with the Westland Sports Club's Second XI. 'I would get a game if either side was short,' Ian recalls, 'and by the time I was nine I decided this was the way I wanted to earn my living.'

At Yeovil's Milford Junior School his games master, Richard Hibbitt, noticed the same quiet dedication, unusual in such a robust, restless boy. Hibbitt also noticed Ian's enormous natural talent. At nine, Ian earned a place in the school's football and cricket teams, each of which was almost totally dominated by eleven-year-olds. Ian fitted in. In football he not only understood the game like a prodigy but, at centre-half, had the power to exploit this knowledge. 'If we had a corner kick, for example, Ian would carefully position himself outside the penalty area,' Hibbitt recalls, 'and once he got the ball, he would head it down neatly then kick a cannon ball into the net. From about 20 yards, too, and when the boy was about nine!'

Young Yeovil bowlers, like any other youngsters, could be a wayward bunch and to reward line and length Hibbitt stacked a pile of pennies six feet down the wicket in front of middle stump. Any boy who scattered the pennies could keep them and young

Ian, the boy wonder: at age nine (above), *with an almost straight bat; and at age ten with his team at Yeovil's Milford Junior School, the season he smashed a ball over the school. Ian is the boy with the bat, second from right, front row.*

Botham, equal to the challenge, earned piles of pennies. Hibbitt also got his young charges in a circle of a radius of eight yards. Standing in the middle, he would throw balls every-which-way at the boys, sharpening their reflexes and slip-fielding skills. This drill, Botham said years later, first whetted his appetite for slip-fielding. Best of all, Hibbitt had a credo for batting. 'If you're going to bother to hit a cricket ball, hit it hard. Don't worry about the school windows.' Ian didn't. He opened up his shoulders and once hit a tape-measure drive that was to become a legend at the school. The team was facing a pacy local boy, a fearsome bowler. Milford School's first wicket went down and Botham came to the crease. He soon smashed a ball, right in the meat of the bat, and stood back to watch it. The ball carried the boundary, the school windows, the school itself and finally landed out of sight, in a far distant playground. 'It was an absolutely *enormous* blow,' Hibbitt remembers, with justified pride, 'it would have been a six at either Taunton or Lord's.' Ian then was ten. He was a star. His father exhorted him onwards. 'Dad always told me that whatever I did today I should do better tomorrow,' Ian recalls. 'It was the *next* event that counted.'

His next sporting conquest took place in London. He was twelve and, travelling to the capital, he competed in a national games programme sponsored by the Crusaders' Union. He entered the Under-13s cricket-ball throw and when called to the line, he threw. The ball sailed up, high over the judges' heads. 'All right, Botham,' shouted a judge, 'you can throw now.' Botham replied that he had already thrown. 'Could you throw again, please,' he was told and Botham, as disgusted then as he is now with inefficiency, took a second, short run and let go. The ball pitched 207 ft 9 ins away, not as far as the first. The record still stands, and with the look of permanency, for it has been converted into metres.

Botham's reputation preceded him to Butler's Mead Secondary School in Yeovil where, big at the age of 13, he was made captain of the Under-16 cricket team. In the same year, he came to the attention of the old Somerset player Bill ('The Hand That Bowled Bradman') Andrews, who looked after the county youth sides. Andrews had never seen such a promising youngster and at 13 Ian made his debut with the Somerset Under-15 side against Wiltshire. It was a memorable match. The captain of the team was Phil Slocombe who later joined Botham at Somerset. 'Ian was a big fellow, a bit tubby,' Slocombe recollects. 'He went in at No. 4 when we were in deep trouble: one run, as I recall, for the loss of two wickets. He threw caution to the wind and started clubbing the ball through the covers. He hit a six over mid-wicket into somebody's garden and by the time he got out, for 80-odd, he had absolutely smashed us out of trouble.' Slocombe, recollecting his precocious team-mate, will admit to something for which Botham has never forgiven him: as a bowler Ian was seen as a joke. 'We didn't much fancy his off-spin or his pace,' Slocombe says, 'so we only put him on to shut him up, and only against tailenders.' To a boy with such a full reservoir of self-confidence, this was painful and baffling and to this day Ian resents, with surprising venom, those who didn't recognise his bowling gifts. 'They had a screwed-up idea that if you were a batsman you were a batsman and if you were a bowler you were a bowler and that was it,' Ian will say; 'there was no such thing as an all-rounder, although I must say, Slocs bloody well bowled and batted but, then, he was captain.'

Peter Roebuck, another future Somerset star, was another member of that Under-15 team. To Roebuck, Botham was something special and memorable. 'My impression of him then, and it's grown since,' recalls Roebuck, 'was that Both was a lively loud-mouth, but full of good humour. If he seemed overbearing it was because he wanted to be part of everything. He always thought he could go out and do this or that and said so at the time. Even today, he will tell you, hand on his heart, that he was a world-class bowler at thirteen. That's an exaggeration.'

It is no exaggeration to say that Ian's early impact on sport was manifold. In badminton, he became the Somerset Under-16s doubles champion and captain of the school's soccer team. Along the way he carved out a reputation as a fiery competitor. 'I never much liked playing anything against Ian, even badminton,' recalls his doubles partner, Robin Trevett, 'and if we were losing a football match 3 nil, with four minutes to go, Ian would still be tackling as hard as he would if we were 1-nil down.'

Ian chiefly was a doer, not a watcher. Yet, he had his heroes. They lay far beyond the boundaries of Somerset. The county side was not without idols: Roy Virgin and, newly from Australia, the dashing Greg Chappell. England were being dramatically served by Ted Dexter and Ken Barrington but, when it came to worship, Ian went straight to the top. 'Gary Sobers was my one cricket hero,' he will say of the great West Indian. 'I wanted to be the next Gary Sobers.'

Similarly, he had no time for Yeovil Town football, nor Swindon Town nor Bournemouth, nor even local Southampton. He was a feverish supporter of the great Chelsea sides of the day: Peter Bonetti, Charlie Cooke, Ron Harris, Peter Osgood, and when Chelsea won the FA Cup in 1970 the walls of his room were painted in Chelsea-blue. The word CHELSEA was stencilled helter-skelter, and hanging like scarves at his window were blue-and-white striped curtains his mother had made. Ian's father remembers taking the boy to a Southampton match at about that time. Ian grudgingly went along, wearing a Chelsea-blue rosette to stand out among the Southampton reds. If Chelsea's Dave Sexton had pursued him as a footballer, Ian might have answered

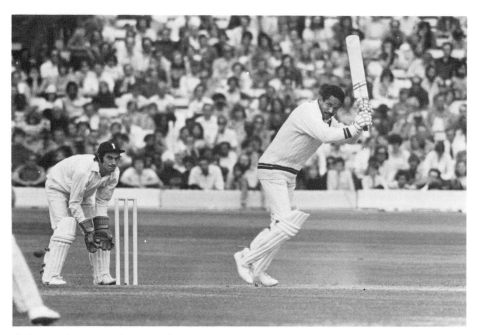

Idol. As a boy, Ian dreamt of emulating one cricketer, the great West Indian, Gary, later Sir Garfield, Sobers.

their call. It was Crystal Palace though who scouted him. Bert Head, the Palace manager of the time, sought and received a report on the Yeovil boy. 'To start with, it was clear to us that Ian wanted to be a winner,' Head recalls, 'and he had all the attributes: ball skills, speed, timing and, above all, enthusiasm. We felt he was a pretty safe bet for the First Division.'

Head phoned Botham's father to offer terms as a professional footballer. Somerset cricket, meanwhile, had registered Botham and, at the age of 15, Ian had reached a crossroads: his career lay in professional sport but which, football or cricket? He and his father discussed the choice. 'In those days, all the glamour and the money seemed to be in football,' Ian recalls, 'but, deep down, we thought I was a better cricketer. Besides, I think I liked the game better.' His enjoyment in cricket went far beyond the pleasures of hitting a ball, even over a schoolhouse, for already he was stimulated by the special, complex challenges offered by cricket. 'What I was beginning to like, and what I like now about cricket,' Botham will say, 'is that in cricket you are a member of a team and, at the same time, you are playing as an individual.' He especially enjoyed the thrilling fear of finality in batting: one mistake and you were out. He laughs, 'Maybe one of the reasons I'm an all-rounder is that I can have a go. If I fail with the bat I know, subconsciously, that I can always redeem myself with the ball.'

Botham picked cricket. Upon leaving school, and while retaining his relations with Somerset, he was taken on by the Lord's ground staff at £12 a week in the spring of

12

1972. It was a joy, the chance of a lifetime, and Ian seized it with both hands. Of the 24 fledgling professionals on the staff, none was more eager than the strapping lad who spent much of the next two seasons rushing between Lord's and Second XI matches for Somerset. 'Once he got his pads on, he'd never take them off,' recalls his Somerset colleague, Keith Jennings, who was with him at Lord's. 'He would get in the nets and pester you to bowl, bowl, bowl. But to be fair, he'd then put you in, and bowl at you for the rest of the day.'

At Lord's, Botham's appetites are still remembered and with awe and affection. Bill Jones, the extrovert 15-stone head boy, later a games master at University College School, Hampstead, remembers Ian's reaction to the ritual hazing of the new boys, a bullying session called 'whiting'. The senior 'A' staff player kept a book in which were entered such 'B' staff misdemeanours as talking back or bowling out a senior boy in the nets. On wet days, or when the elder boys otherwise felt bored, 'whitings' took place. The older boys would go *en masse* to the 'B' changing room and there, drawing up benches, they would quietly encircle the young players. One by one, the names of the hapless 'B' staff were rung out. One by one, older boys would pass judgement in Stentorian voices. 'No' – and a young 'B' staff player would be acquitted of some known or unknown crime. 'Yes' – and they would be on him, swarming over the luckless miscreant and pinning him down, shoulders and knees, onto a treatment table. The victim would then be stripped and his crutch painted with whitewash. He was thereafter graded, from 0 to 10, according to how stoutly he fought back. Botham, struggling like a lion against the overwhelming weight of perhaps a dozen assailants, recorded the most consistently high marks in ground staff history.

Ian also got full marks when the Lord's Nippers, the name of the team, gathered with medical students of St Mary's Hospital after a match. The students had among their numbers, they thought, a wondrous drinker who could quaff down a 'yard of ale' without stopping. Botham, aged 16, watched the feat, stepped forward and did the same thing, saving face for the Nippers. The coaches, Len Muncer and Harry Sharp, like the players, seemed baffled by Botham. 'Frankly, I didn't think he would become the player he has,' admits Sharp. 'He had the enthusiasm but I thought he would make only a good, average county cricketer.' Clearly, Botham had the raw, wilful skills, but he lacked the elegance. In the matches with clubs, schools and hospitals he rarely got past 50. Muncer remembers an MCC match against a weak City of London School side. Ian was told to get out after reaching 50. When Ian passed his half-century, he ignored shouts to desist and only upon reaching his 100 did he get out. As a bowler, Botham got short shrift; it was felt that there were at least five more promising young bowlers on the staff, but by the end of the following summer Muncer was forced to revise his judgement. He wrote this report: 'A very outstanding cricketer who shows a great deal of promise but does everything in his own way. He needs a lot of guidance and is proving better with the bat than the ball, possibly because he has not had a great deal of opportunity, although in the course of time will prove to be a more than useful bowler.'

Muncer's prophecy, unknown to Botham, was shared notably by one man: Tom Cartwright, the artful former Warwickshire and England medium-pacer, who was now coaching at Millfield and playing for Somerset. Cartwright, a rebel himself, saw Ian then as all of cricket later was to see him: 'He is a breath of fresh air. He is larger than life.' Cartwright, together with such wise county heads as the future umpire Ken

Palmer and coach Peter Robinson, entered into the training of Botham, the bowler. Botham vividly recalls those sessions. They worked on the basics of bowling: an economical run-up, accuracy, use of the seam and, mostly, the use of his body more than his arm in delivering the ball. Cartwright also restrained Botham: 'You've got the strength but not the action of a top-level pace bowler. Don't try to accelerate, you'll destroy your rhythm and burn yourself out.'

Botham played his first match for Somerset First XI on September 2, 1973, the same week that he finished his training with the Lord's ground staff. The season was nearly over, nothing was at stake. He was picked to play in the John Player League game against Sussex at Hove. It was an unremarkable debut – lbw for two and 22 runs without a wicket in his bowling spell – except for a striking catch he took at deep backward square leg. 'The batsman went for a big hit, didn't get hold of it and skied it. I ran in, dived full-length, and caught the ball just as I hit the ground,' Botham recalls. 'It wasn't a bad catch.' It was a significant one too, in retrospect: the batsman was Tony Greig, the man Botham one day was to succeed as the key all-rounder for England. Botham also played the following Sunday against Surrey at the Oval and, here again, he gives us something to remember him by: his first top-class wicket. 'It was a crap ball, full toss,' Botham remembers, 'but I trapped him leg before wicket.' The batsman was Geoff Howarth, the New Zealand player who would give him so much trouble in future Test matches.

The next season, 1974, was – to use the word advisedly – a bumper year for Botham. It was the summer he was blooded by Andy Roberts, coming to fame in the quarter-final Benson and Hedges tie between Somerset and Hampshire on June 12 at Taunton. Botham had played in only four first-class fixtures that year and had little to show for it: an innings of 26 and only a single wicket at the cost of 144 runs in 50 overs. Still, at very nearly the last minute Close named him in the side for the crucial match. Hampshire batted first and, after floundering, put up a passable total of 182 runs with Botham, a first-change bowler, taking two satisfying wickets, those of the great Barry Richards and Peter Sainsbury, and yielding only 33 runs.

In reply, Somerset stumbled to 113 for seven when young Botham came in. His partner, Cartwright, skied the next ball to deep mid-on – out – and sent the huge home crowd into gloom. Somerset: 113 for eight, with 70 runs needed off the remaining 15 overs. Botham soon clubbed a towering six over square leg, and with Hallam Moseley pushing singles at the other end the score climbed to 131 when the dreaded Roberts, then the scourge from Antigua, was again given the ball. An ugly lifter from Roberts, which Botham was shaping to hook, soon shattered the youngster's back teeth, dropping him like a sack of grain to the ground. 'I spat out blood and a couple of broken teeth and the lads brought me a glass of water,' Botham was later to recall, lucidly, as in a slow motion film. 'I shook myself and felt fine. As I look back on it, hitting me in the mouth was the worst thing Andy could have done. It seemed to relax me. It made me all the keener. The next ball, he tried the obvious thing, a yorker, and I stood back and clipped it for three.' The rest is history: the last ball before the final over, which was to be bowled by Roberts, was smashed by Botham to the boundary to bring him his 45th run and Somerset an astonishing triumph over Hampshire. Botham was engulfed by fans – not for the last time – and won the Gold Award. The next morning England had a new cricketing hero. A star was born. Ian has kept one of the newspaper headlines of the day. It reads simply: 'Blood, Sweat and Cheers.'

14

Blooded. Botham, eighteen, came of age in 1974 during the Benson and Hedges quarter-final tie against Hampshire at Taunton. Felled by Andy Roberts, he recovered and woke up a hero.

It also was the summer he met Kathryn Waller, in the rain at Leicester, during the Benson and Hedges tie that followed the heroics at Taunton. She was there with her sister, down to see the family friend, Close, and his Somerset side. 'I didn't know Ian was a cricketer and he didn't tell me when I met him,' she recalls. 'About all I can remember was that he was quiet and nice and he helped me find my car in the rain.' They dined that evening and, although his celebrated jaw was still sore, Ian was modest and made no allusion to it.

Botham prospered under Close that summer, although they sometimes were at loggerheads. Both being combustible characters, sparks flew. This happened, for example, during a Gillette Cup match against Surrey that summer at Taunton. Botham was bowling. A ball was hit back down the wicket and he twisted to grab it. The non-striking batsman unwisely went for a quick single and both batsmen finished at the far end. All Botham needed to do was to walk to the stumps and lift off the bails. Instinctively, though, he wheeled round and threw the stumps down from some five yards. Close blew up. He shouted at Ian for being such a bloody fool. Ian shouted back. Their anger echoed round the county ground. 'It was quite amusing,' Ian later recalled. 'We used to have our rows, but at the end we'd come out of the dressing-room and go into the bar and be the first to buy each other a drink. That's why some people didn't get on with Closey. They would have a row, take umbrage and sulk for a week, whereas we would blow up and forget it. Closey did me a lot of good. A lot of my confidence comes from Closey. I've never seen him scared. In fact, I think he went over the top sometimes to prove how brave he was, when he needn't have done it.'

But the end of the summer, aged 18, Botham had secured his place once and for all in the Somerset side by finishing his season with promising figures: 441 runs, with a highest score of 59, for an average of 16·96; 30 wickets at the cost of 779 runs and a best innings of 5–59 and fifteen catches. At Christmas, he and Kathryn became engaged, to the distress of Close.

Through the winter, Botham built himself up while working at a building site in Yeovil, but in 1975 the cricket stood still. 'He tried to make things happen that year,' Close recalls, 'and things don't always happen in cricket.' Cartwright, in his last season with the county side, was busy teaching Botham restraint, trying to shackle him within the bounds of medium-fast bowling. Mike Brearley, the Middlesex captain, was having an ambivalent second look at the unmeasured young star. 'One minute he would look a big whacker of the ball, not very cultured,' he recalls, 'and the next he would play this mature, controlled shot. I didn't know what to make of him.' In Taunton, Botham was enjoying his last summer as a bachelor with his old room-mate, Dennis Breakwell, the bowler. 'There were a few takeaway Indian dinners that summer,' recalls Breakwell, 'and a few evenings in the pub. In those days, we didn't have much money and Both would take bets that he could drink three pints of beer in under a minute. It was worse than robbing a bank.' At each end of the season, Botham was playing centre-forward in the Somerset Senior League. 'He didn't need a football,' recalls Trevor Gard, the reserve wicket-keeper for Somerset. 'He'd just kick you in the backside, straight up in the air.' Botham nevertheless retained his secure place in the Somerset side in 1975, although his end-of-term report could have been better: 584 First XI runs and 62 wickets.

That autumn, Botham did not return to his building site job in Yeovil. He went north and, living at Thorne in Yorkshire with his future in-laws, worked as a sales

16

representative for Gerry Waller's firm, Promuco, makers of quality musical drums and drumsticks. Travelling in a battered car, the back loaded down with goods, Ian covered an enormous area from Aberdeen to Portsmouth. He never took no for an answer. Waller recalls a time when a Northampton music shop manager told Ian he neither wanted any drumsticks nor had heard of Promuco. 'Well, you've heard of us now,' Botham replied. 'Would you like any drumsticks?' The man resisted the hard sell and Botham took a scathing look round the shop. 'To tell you the truth,' he said, 'seeing this scruffy place, I wouldn't sell anything to you anyway,' and walked out. Waller is still amused by the incident. 'I didn't know whether to laugh or fire him,' he recalls, 'but the upshot was, the next time Ian went round, the fellow bought the drumsticks.'

Botham bought an old cottage in nearby Epworth and, marrying Kathryn in January of 1976, they moved in and began restoring it. In cricket, 1976 was also to be a landmark year. In May, batting at number eight in a championship match at Hove, he savaged Tony Greig and the other Sussex bowlers for 97 runs, his highest score to date, and by midsummer, elevated to number four by captain Close, he had hammered out his maiden century on an amiable batting strip at Trent Bridge. He scored 116 runs in boundaries – 6 sixes and 20 fours – before Somerset declared with Botham on 167 not out. 'What a cocky begger he was that day,' recalls Derek Randall, who himself scored an unbeaten 204 in the match. 'He opened up by pulling a ball for six. He went on to play one of the best innings I've ever seen in my life.'

Botham flourished that summer for, at last, he was out from under the long shadow of his fierce friendly rival in the Somerset team, Viv Richards. Richards was playing with the powerful West Indies team which were mauling England as, incidentally, Andy Roberts took his 100th Test wicket to set a future target for the young all-rounder at Somerset. Botham played against Richards three times that season and he remembers, vividly, each of the encounters. He stopped Richards at 51, adroitly caught behind in the county match at Taunton. Best of all, his friend was there when Botham played his first two representative appearances for England: the first and third Prudential Trophy one-day games. The first was at Scarborough. England went in and Botham, batting number seven, didn't last long: after scoring a single run, he was out, trying to hook a ball from Michael Holding. The West Indies, in reply to England's 202 runs, were soon coasting along comfortably with Richards scoring freely. 'When Viv reached his century, I went up to congratulate him and he smiled at me. "Man," he said, "You go back there and bowl. I'm not playing for Somerset now, I'm playing for West Indies."'

If the batting of Richards has always been a challenge, so too has the all-round skill of the South African Mike Procter, of Gloucestershire. Botham's cricketing life is full of dark little incidents, affronts and defeats, and he encourages them to fester in some remote fold of his mind. Such an incident concerns Procter. In fact, it turns round a single ball bowled by the South African in a county match on the first day of June that summer at Taunton. Somerset scored 333 runs, bowled out Gloucestershire for 79 and asked the visitors to follow on. Gloucestershire did, handsomely scoring 372, despite Botham's exhausting 37·1-over effort that earned him five wickets and brought his match total to his best ever, eleven. Somerset's target of 119 looked a cinch as Rose and Slocombe reached 43 without loss. Wickets then began to fall. When Botham came in with the score 100 for six, Somerset still looked secure. Suddenly Botham was gone. Bowled. By Procter. By an awkward little off-spinner. Years later, driving

Somerset cap. Ian receives his county lid from Somerset captain Brian Close at a West Indies match in Taunton on May 26, 1976.

through the mild green Somerset countryside, Botham's knuckles went white on the steering wheel as he recalled the ball. 'I don't mind getting out to Procky bowling seamers because they're his forte,' he said. 'But the last thing I want to do is to get out to him bowling off-spin. Off-spin! *Procter*!' The ball had been made all the more mortifying when Somerset went on to lose that match by eight runs.

All in all it had been a memorable year, full of peaks and valleys, and in it Botham had come of age. He had been married, capped by Somerset and blooded by England. He had scored his first century, knocked over eleven rival wickets in a match and fulfilled his promise. His statistics, counting the county and international games, first-class and one-day, were worthy of attention: 1,471 runs, 101 wickets and 19 catches. They drew attention too, and Ian was rewarded that winter with a Whitbread Trust 'scholarship' to Australia. It was not a wholly gratifying trip, for he played only a handful of grade matches in Melbourne, none against class competition, most of them ruined by rain.

In fact, the only impact Botham made upon the Australians was with his right fist. The incident took place one evening in the 'MCG', a bar near the Melbourne Cricket Ground. Botham was sitting with Ian Chappell when the former Australian captain raised rude doubts over the quality of English cricket: the Poms, after all, recently had been slaughtered by the same West Indian Test side that had been smashed 5–1 by the Australians. Botham disagreed with the judgement. Chappell persisted. Botham suggested he shut up. Chappell didn't. Botham stood up and with one blow knocked Chappell off his bar stool and flat onto the floor. Chappell dusted himself off and said

18

nothing. The matter was dropped until, upon departing, Chappell turned at the door and cast another aspersion on England. That did it. Botham was up like a shot. He chased Chappell out into the street, vaulted a parked car and luckily for both men, lost his prey in the traffic.

As for sport, while in Melbourne Ian learned to surf in the sea and worked on his bowling with Frank Tyson, who, at 46, could still teach an attentive lad a thing or two about cricket. 'Tyson taught me that on fast Australian wickets I shouldn't bowl my out-swingers at the stumps,' Botham recalls, 'I should bowl them to move away towards first slip.' The tip was to help Ian in future trips to Australia.

THREE

Enter Botham

The England changing-room at Lord's is reached by entering the pavilion through the main doors, climbing a short flight of stairs, turning right at the Long Room, surmounting two more flights of stairs, turning right down a corridor of offices and a physiotherapist's room and at the end making a left through a banged-up old door marked No Admittance Unless by Personal Invitation by Captain or the Manager. The changing-room is comfortably drab with wash basins on the right-hand wall, two generous windows dead ahead and, between these windows, a pair of glass doors leading on to a wrought-iron balcony. The balcony commands a sudden, stunning view of the most famous cricket ground in the world.

The changing-room is furnished with wonderful junk. In the centre is a huge wooden kitchen table, cluttered with letters, telegrams and benefit bats to be signed. Beside the balcony door stands an old dressing table, probably of Edwardian origin, with rickety legs and a cumbersome swinging mirror. This is where Geoffrey Boycott has taken up his place for years. Across the balcony threshold, opposite Boycott, is a folding metal chair where Mike Brearley sits, snapping open the *Guardian* or perhaps *The Times* for a glance at the news. Bob Taylor is back in a far corner, near a wash basin. Tidy wicket-keeper that he is, Taylor is setting up house to keep his gear clean and in order over the next six days.

All is well in the England camp; everyone has his place and there is a place for everyone. Cricketers, like any other sportsmen, have the habit of staking out a spot in a changing-room and forever returning to it. They follow this habit to establish and retain order, or perhaps to court luck. Or perhaps, driven by some deeper unease, they seek to create an air of territorial imperative that will serve to warn others against taking their place on the team. Sir Leonard Hutton, while clearly unchallenged for his place, did not observe the captain's custom of taking the spot nearest the action on the field, as Brearley does by the balcony. Sir Leonard chose to sit on an over-stuffed sofa under one of the big windows. He grew accustomed to this sofa over the years, he will explain, much as he has the chair in his sitting-room at home. While sitting on the changing-room sofa, though, Sir Leonard rarely would watch the cricket through the big window. 'In actual fact, watching cricket through glass is not good. It distorts your view,' he will explain. 'I wouldn't look through a window. Never. I would be outside or inside; looking through the open door.'

Botham enters the room with his bat, and Hendrick. They are among the last to

Gathering at Grace Gate at Lord's: (left to right) *brother Graeme, mother Marie, son Liam, father Les, wife and daughter Kathryn and Sarah, father-in-law Gerry Waller, mother-in-law Jan, sister-in-law Lindsay and her fiancé Paul Southall. Missing were Ian's sisters, Dale Wise, who was having a baby, and Wendy, at work in Yeovil.*

arrive. Most bowlers prefer not to come early to a ground and this, in the case of such an eager cricketer as Botham, may seem strange. Ian has his reasons. 'If I come early, and England's batting, I've got to sit around all day and watch other people play cricket and that frustrates me,' he will say, then grin. 'On the other hand, if we're bowling, I'm frustrated if I can't get on with it *straightaway.*'

Botham nevertheless is much at home in this changing-room. After all, it was the scene of his first international match, the MCC game against the Australians on May 25–27, 1977. Hendrick remembers the morning of practice, just before that game, and how Botham vented his nervous energy in the changing-room. There were baseball gloves lying round the room which somehow had been got hold of from the Australians who often practise with them. Botham and Hendrick put on the gloves and began playing catch with a cricket ball. The ball flew between them, faster and faster, the pace quickening as Botham's pent-up adrenalin burst its banks. The players soon were on collision course and the other players, tying their shoe laces, looked up to follow the increasingly intemperate battle of wills. Neither man would back down. The battle was becoming dangerous when Botham, in an inspired act of face-saving, suddenly let loose and sent the ball whistling safely past Hendrick's head. The ball rifled off the far wall and clattered round the room. The cricketers fell silent. Someone called a halt to the game, but not before Botham had left his mark literally, symbolically – and perhaps with subconscious intent – on the changing-room wall at Lord's. It could be found for months afterwards, a mark at about eye-level, over near the door. It is now covered in paint.

Symbolically and actually, Botham leaves his mark. In fact, Roy Harrington, who has been the Lord's changing-room attendant for forty years, recalls vividly the morning of Ian's Lord's Test debut, against Pakistan in 1978. 'He walked through the door and paused a moment to look around the room,' remembers Harrington. 'Then he made a bee-line for the far sofa under the window. That was to be his place, and that was the end of it.' The sofa, of course, was Sir Leonard's old stuffed sofa. Botham didn't know this at the time and now sniffs at any ironical significance in his choice. Botham is not a man to read omens. He is a straight-up-and-down fellow, but to say he is not superstitious is not altogether true. For instance, he is a man who pulls on his right trouser leg before his left yet, later in the Test, will purposely put on his left batting pad before his right one. Botham is not keen to discuss this superstition, for he likes to see himself as master of his own fate. 'The pad thing is just a habit,' he will say, rather impatiently. 'I've only become aware of doing it in the last couple of years.'

Botham, on Hutton's sofa, before the first morning's play against India in 1979, lights a cigarette, Harrington brings him a cup of tea and, in turn, Botham asks a favour of the dutiful attendant. Will Harrington roll an extra grip on Ian's new bat? Harrington takes the bat and retreats to his little ante-room while Botham, collecting his wits, sits quietly smoking and sipping his tea. Unavoidably, like a tongue to a cavity, his thoughts return to the 100-wicket Test record of Roberts' and, just as unavoidably, to the faint memory of being hit in the mouth, five summers ago, by the thunderbolt flung down by Roberts in the Benson and Hedges match at Taunton. *Suddenly the ball was on me. I managed to get my hand up and it was my fist, I think, that smashed out my teeth. My first reaction was disbelief: Christ Almighty, I never saw a ball come so quick in my life*. Botham sees no coincidence in the fact that the man who blooded him as a young star of cricket is the same man whose Test record he is aiming to shatter.

The cricket case at Botham's feet is one of the heaviest in the game for, as an all-rounder, he needs the specialist equipment of both batsman and bowler. A dozen pairs of socks; a single pair to be worn while batting, two pairs to cushion his feet while bowling, three pairs if the ground is especially hard for bowling. Six shirts. Six vests. Five pairs of flannels. Three sweaters: one long-sleeved, two short-sleeved. A bag of odds and sods: sweat bands, foot creams, boot stud keys, a Venalin Spray dispenser for the rare attack of exercise asthma. A pair of batting pads. Three bats. Two pairs of batting shoes, one with and one without studs: 'Brears gets furious when I wear the ones without the studs. He thinks I slip in them and, in fact, I *want* to slip. I want to slide and turn, like a tennis player.' A pair of heavy bowler's boots, which due to their durability and weight are called 'diving boots' among cricketers. Botham's diving boots are built up half an inch in the heels to take stress off his Achilles tendons. 'John Lever bowls in ordinary batting boots,' Botham points out, ruefully; 'he's lucky, he's light on his feet.'

Botham also has a pair of light training shoes which, at the moment, he is wearing as England go out for exercises with Bernard Thomas and a turn in the nets. 'Basically, I don't like nets all that much,' he will say, 'I feel closed in and the atmosphere is artificial. I only bat because I want to feel the ball on the bat.' He bats for only ten minutes. He attacks so savagely that Phil Edmonds won't bowl at him because he is fed up with chasing balls smashed past him. Botham bowls perhaps a dozen balls. One is his new experimental slow ball which, predictably, skids high and wide along the net.

Botham laughs, disgusted with himself. A good deceptive slow ball is the one ball he feels is missing from his armoury. It is a difficult ball to master: in delivery, the bowler must neither reduce the speed of his run-up nor the speed at which his arm comes over. On the recommendation of Brian Close, when Botham played under his captaincy for Somerset, Botham sought advice on this problem from the former Australian Test bowler, Neil Hawke, who now lives in Lancashire.

Hawke, in turn, learned his slow ball from Alan McGilvray, the commentator, who in a season in the 1930s took about 18 first-class wickets with it. Hawke was even more successful: of his 91 Test wickets, taken between 1962 and 1968, about 30 were attributed to the cunning slow ball. The method is a devil to master. Hawke explained it to Botham: the bowler holds the ball in an orthodox fashion, with the first two fingers, the 'driving fingers', on top. The seam is tilted about 70 degrees away from the fingers which, if seen by the batsman, will give the illusion of an in-swinger or perhaps a leg-cutter.

The trick comes in bowling the ball. Hawke explained: 'The two driving fingers, instead of projecting from behind the ball to push it forwards and give it its normal momentum, now must slide loosely across the ball towards the thumb and in the direction of gully as the arm comes down. The ball will continue, one hopes, on the same course towards the batsman, but at a greatly reduced speed.' Botham has practised Hawke's slow ball, but as yet has not achieved sufficient control to use it in battle, even in meaningless moments of a county match.

At 11 a.m. Botham is back in the changing-room with the rest of the side, save Mike Brearley. Brearley has gone to the middle to toss with the Indian captain, Srinivasaraghavan Venkataraghavan, who, mercifully, is known only as Venkat. 'There is nothing nicer than to see the coin come down and Brears walk over to the groundsman and tell him which roller he wants,' says Botham, 'because then we know we've won the toss and we're batting.' The players can see from the balcony that there is some confusion over the toss this time, but clearly England has lost it. Lever, Botham, Hendrick, Miller instinctively glance at the heavy, phlegmy sky. 'Do you think it's going to swing today?' Botham asks to no one in particular and, as in a litany, no one in particular replies: 'It swung a little in the nets.'

There now is less than thirty minutes to go. Botham changes into his diving boots, joins most of his mates in the lavatory for a last visit before returning to his sofa for a last cigarette. He tries to read the newspaper but anxiety bunches in his belly. One thought is in his mind and, try as he might, it won't go away. The 100th wicket will come, he thinks, *let's get it today*. He stands and does a few shoulder-rolls. When the team starts together out of the door, Ian shouts: 'Let's go!' Then, in a moment of unrestraint, he blurts out: 'A bottle of champagne to the man who catches my 100th wicket!' His offer is met by silence as England clatter down the stairs. Botham feels he is lucky, for he is equal to the big occasion and his nervousness lifts the moment his feet touch the field. As St Andrews is to the golfer, Covent Garden to the opera singer, so Lord's is to the cricket star. 'Lord's is the place,' Ian will say, moved to lyricism, 'and when I'm here, God seems to say to me, "Don't worry, lad, you'll be all right."' Further, Botham is an actor, in that he is sustained by an audience, and for this reason he is inspired at Lord's. 'I like Lord's better than the other Test grounds,' he will say, 'the crowd seems to be nearer there, and I feel I can get among them.' His bowling record so far at Mecca: two Tests (Pakistan and New Zealand), 19 wickets.

Lever and Botham will open the bowling, Lever from the Pavilion End and Botham, as is his custom, from the Nursery End. Botham is happy down there: he reckons that in his two previous Tests, together with assorted one-day internationals and many Somerset matches, he has bowled no more than a dozen overs from the Pavilion End. The field at Lord's slopes some seven feet from the grandstand to the Tavern side of the ground – four of those feet across the square of 14 wickets – and bowling from the Nursery End Botham can make use of this right-to-left slope. It helps him avoid running down the wicket after his delivery, and, more important, it complements his stock ball, an out-swinger to the right-hander, hurrying it along. 'It's not a huge slope,' Botham will say, 'but as you bowl on it you feel yourself go, and it's a lot smoother.'

India know little about Botham. Bishen Bedi, the former Northamptonshire captain, is the only member of the side who has seen much of the young Englishman. The elder statesman among the Indians, Bedi spoke of Botham at the team meeting on the eve of the first Test, at Edgbaston. 'Ian is not satisfied to just beat the bat. He is an attacking bowler and he will keep the slips busy for the out-swinger,' Bedi had said. 'He is very, very experimental and he is going to look for a wicket off every ball. So be patient. His in-swinger is not all that accurate. I don't think his bouncer is a wicket-taking ball. It is not quick enough and it bounces in his half of the wicket, so you can see it coming. Ian bowls a lot of rubbish that goes unpunished. If we are good enough to wait for the loose deliveries we can get runs off him.'

India apparently took little heed of Bedi's advice in that Edgbaston Test. They scored 156 runs off him, costly enough, but in turn Botham raked their ranks for seven wickets. One of his victims had been Chetan Chauhan, the mild little opener from Delhi, who seemed to disprove Bedi's belief that one can see Botham's bouncer on its way in. Chauhan certainly hadn't done so in the first innings. He had turned his head away from one, only the eighth ball he received, got an awkward touch, and popped an easy catch to Graham Gooch in the slips. Botham, now at Lord's, sees Chauhan and his opening partner Sunil Gavaskar make their way on to the field. He watches Chauhan. 'You're not exactly *afraid* of bouncers,' he thinks of the Indian, 'you're just not interested in them. You'll turn your head away, won't you?' Botham's chemistry of combat is at work: fix a man in your mind, reduce him, feel your dominance rise over him. Botham will think at a batsman: 'I've got the ball. I'm going to get you out.'

The umpires for the game are Dicky Bird, now taking his place at the Pavilion End, and Ken Palmer, down at the Nursery End. In his pockets, Palmer carries the typical umpire's paraphernalia: a pen-knife, a booklet of the rules and regulations, a pen and card for notes, a light-meter, a cloth to clean the ball. He also carries a replacement ball, one about 15 overs old (Bird has one of about 40 overs old), for use if the opening

Bishen Bedi

25

ball loses its shape or, improbably, if it is lost in the crowd. Palmer also carries six key-ring ornaments, miniature Watney Red beer barrels; he uses them to count deliveries by changing them, one at a time, from one pocket to the other as balls are bowled. Finally, he carries a white metal ring, the bowler's marker, which he now places on the turf behind the middle stump.

Lever bowls the first over, without drama. It is Botham's turn. He has picked up the metal ring from behind the stump, taken one giant step, then a dozen more full, measured strides to the spot for his mark. He places the ring down in a line with the middle stump. With his boot he paws a line. He then continues five more yards, turns and, without pausing, starts in. Botham knows his first ball will be a loosener, well outside the off stump, and that he will not have worked up a full head of steam by the end of the first over. Beyond this, he has only a vague plan of attack. He likes to keep it this way, vague. When he is in perfect, creative rhythm, he will not know what kind of ball he will bowl – in-swinger, out-swinger, bouncer, yorker, whatever – until perhaps three strides before the point of delivery. In this regard, he is a genuine, creative artist, working with controlled impulse. 'When you're bowling well, you don't worry, you just *do* it – whatever comes into your mind,' he will say. 'If *I'm* not sure of the ball I'm going to bowl, how the hell is the batsman going to guess it?'

Chauhan, for his part, is nervy. Bedi had said one could see Botham's bouncer and at Edgbaston Chauhan had not seen it. Chauhan tells himself he's not afraid of the Englishman's bouncer. Instead, the Indian tries to convince himself that Botham's danger ball is the swift out-swinger which, in the damp, heavy weather, might leap erratically away from the bat. The battle is joined. At the other end, Gavaskar also is batting with some discomfort, first against Lever, then Botham. As the overs tick past, Botham grows annoyed, baffled by the ball's curious behaviour. In the slips, as Lever bowls, Botham speaks of the problem with Brearley and Taylor. 'The odd ball swings and the next one doesn't,' he says. Brearley suggests he is trying too hard. Taylor says not to fight it, the cause is the moisture in the air.

Moisture, indeed, is in the air, and falling. Rain soon halts play for 18 minutes, then again for 12 minutes and as the Test moves into the afternoon Botham is still in his first spell, only just worked up to his full pace. The Indians are frustrated by the rain and the unpredictable behaviour of the ball. They have only 12 runs on the board when Botham again is bowling at Chauhan. Botham comes in. The ball, resting lightly on the fingertips of both hands, is shifted into the right hand some eight yards from the crease. Chauhan is looking out for the unruly out-swinger. The notion of a bouncer flits through Botham's mind but suddenly, unaccountably, he has bowled something else: an in-swinger of full length. It is an amiable ball, fat for the hitting. Chauhan, however, has committed himself towards the off stump. The ball pitches near his feet, near middle and leg, and races further down the leg side. The Indian is overbalanced. He is in a tangle. He makes a wristy little flick at the ball, part in defence and part in attack. The ball shoots just behind square leg. Randall, quick as a blink, hands forward and falling, scoops it up cleanly. Chauhan is disgusted with himself. 'It wasn't a wicket-taking ball,' he is to say afterwards. 'I shouldn't have played it.' Botham concurs. Yes, it was a bad-ball wicket. He does not smile: bad balls take wickets, too. Chauhan is gone: India are 12 for one.

Botham bowls throughout the first session and shortly before lunch he nearly has Gavaskar, edging a ball past his leg stump. Botham toils on. John Arlott is

Test wicket No. 95. The India opener Chetan Chauhan, tangled up by an in-swinger, flicks a ball to Randall behind square leg.

commentating on BBC Radio 3. 'Botham. Straight in his run as a shire horse,' he says in his gravelly Hampshire accent, and indeed there is Botham's run-in, etched nearly string-straight on the damp grass. At the other end, meanwhile, Hendrick has replaced Lever and this puts Botham in a good frame of mind. 'If I had my choice of bowling with anybody at the other end, it would be Hendo,' he will say. 'He is the most accurate bowler in the world and that suits me. He *hates* to give away runs. After a batsman is tied down for a while off Hendo, he'll try to break out and score off me.'

Botham is in his favourite fielding position, second slip. He loves fielding in a close cordon. 'A lot of bowlers want to go out to fine leg and forget it all,' he says, 'I want to stay involved in the game. At slip, you learn a lot about your own bowlers and also you can study the batsmen.' So involved does Botham become in the slips, so engrossed in the action, that he actually inches closer and closer to the bat; like a child in a sweet shop. There is no class slip-fielder in the game who gets as near to the bat as Botham. At first slip, Brearley signals him back. Botham feels a brief flair of anger. It is Botham's nature to resist instructions, even from a man he admires, and in childish response he picks mud from his boot and flips it onto the ground in front of his captain. Brearley smiles. He is amused by his rebellious boy and, not for the first time, he clears his patch of the bits of mud. 'When Ian stands next to me,' he laughs later, 'I spend a lot of time gardening. But you may have noticed that once he made his gesture of defiance, he *did* move back.'

27

Botham's conduct in the slips at times annoys Hendrick as well. The Somerset all-rounder, Hendrick feels, doesn't appear to be concentrating as he stands there, hands on knees. Worse, hands on knees, Botham is not observing the golden rule of slip-fielding: stay down in a crouch and you will be in position to take the low catch or rise to meet a rising ball. In standing as he does, half up, Botham often finds himself reflexively sinking and rising to take a catch. Botham, of course, has a ready answer to Hendrick's criticism: 'I don't like to crouch. Maybe it's because I'm tired and aching after bowling.' A second golden rule of slip-fielding, at least at second slip, says: watch the bat. Botham here again violates the rule, for sometimes he watches the bat and sometimes ('when I'm lazy') he watches the ball's journey from bowler to batsman. This may not be such a heinous crime, since Graham Roope, a former England colleague of Botham's and one of the finest close fielders in the game, is a ball-watcher.

The score is 23 for one wicket. Hendrick is bowling at Dilip Vengsarkar, the tall and elegant young man from Bombay who, after two overs, is still to get off the mark. First ball, Hendrick bangs in a short one and the Indian, half-fending, ticks a low chance towards Botham. Botham bobs down and brilliantly accepts it, left handed. Hendrick, leaping forward, has to grin: bloody hell, he thinks, absolutely typical: a wonderful catch by Botham, done wrong. India is now 23 for two and, not surprisingly, Botham has had a hand in both wickets.

India are bogged down. Shortly after lunch they lose their third wicket, the valued one of Gundappa Viswanath, the tiny veteran with the lugubrious look and the wrap-around beard: caught Brearley, bowled Hendrick for 21. India: 51 for three. Vish's wicket is followed soon by another equally vital one, that of Gavaskar. At the crease for two hours and 19 minutes for his 42 runs, Gavaskar is stalled, tied down by Hendrick, and a little rashly he tries to cut a nipping-away ball from Gooch and is caught behind. India: 75 for four.

Botham, after consultations with his captain, abandons the frustrating Nursery End, moves to the Pavilion End. His second wicket of the day, the 96th in his Test career, is soon to fall. The victim, the bespectacled Anshuman Gaekwad, who has played against every major cricketing country in his career, has high regard for Botham: quite apart from the Somerset bowler's swing in the air, Gaekwad feels no one in the world, *no one*, can get a ball to move as much off the wicket. He has been in for more than one and a half hours and, alternately pinned down by Hendrick and assaulted by Botham, he has been able to squeeze out only a dozen runs. Botham has read the Indian's anxiety and he is peppering him with in-swingers, one after another and then, at the last moment of the next delivery, he chooses an out-swinger. The ball pitches just short of a length, holds up a bit, lifts off the 'ridge', swings wide. Gaekwad is befuddled. 'I was about to leave it,' he is to say later, 'but suddenly it came up and, at the last moment, I pushed at it.' Gaekwad gets a touch. The ball races off the edge of the bat – straight to Taylor. Gaekwad is gone. India: 79 for five.

(Weeks later, Botham sat in a hotel room and watched the replay of the fall of Gaekwad's wicket over a television video-tape. Jim Laker was commentating. 'Not a very good delivery. Not a very good shot,' Laker had said to thousands of BBC viewers. 'But they all go down in the book.' Replayed on tape, as though for Botham's benefit, it had sounded oddly rude. Botham stiffened and asked for the tape to be backed-up and the fall of the wicket shown again. It was and, once again, Laker was dismissive about Botham's delivery and repeated that all wickets went into the book.

Got it. Vengsarkar is caught, left hand and low down, by Botham off the bowling of Hendrick in the Second Test at Lord's.

'You're goddam right they do, Jim,' Botham had snapped at the set, 'they all go down in the book.')

Kapil Dev is the next to go down in the book. He is to be Botham's third wicket of the day, his 97th in 19 Tests. Kapil Dev is a natural rival to Botham. Cornhill, the Test sponsors, describe him in their brochure: 'Kapil Dev (20, Haryawa). India's answer to Ian Botham, may not in fact be quite as formidable an all-round talent as the Somerset man but is undoubtedly his country's best find for many years . . . a clean-driving right-handed batsman.' Kapil Dev hasn't been doing much clean-driving off Botham in the series, twice falling to him cheaply at Edgbaston (for 1 and 21), and now has scored four runs and played at all the four balls he received. Botham recognises the fault in such fervour. Kapil Dev must be asked to play at a bad ball. Botham pounds in and delivers just such a ball: an out-swinger, widish, and Kapil Dev lunges after it. The ball shoots off a thick edge, low and well to the right of Geoff Miller in fourth slip. Miller flings himself down, tumbles, comes up with an astonishing catch. Kapil Dev pauses in disbelief before moving off towards the pavilion. India: 89 for six.

Botham, the England steamroller, soon is to stall over the young Punjabi, Yashpal Sharma, who is making his Test debut and batting with deliberation. He has been in nearly an hour, received 52 balls and scored eleven runs. As Botham, bowling, turns and starts in, young Sharma backs away and holds up his hand. Umpire Palmer comes forward. The Indian says there is something in his eye. He asks if he can go off to have it looked after. Brearley, on the spot, is a hard man under such circumstances: he firmly protests that Sharma must stay on. 'You can go off if you like,' Palmer tells the young Indian, 'but if you do, we'll have another batsman.'

Boycott by now has arrived on the scene and, examining Sharma's eye, declares there is nothing in it and suggests they get on with the match. India send on a man to wash out their batsman's eye. England, fed up with the time being wasted, increase the pressure by making a great casual show of indifference over the delay. Players sit down, chew grass. Hendrick, Gooch, Miller and David Gower settle down in a circle. 'A quick game of knock-out whist?' asks Hendrick. Someone asks who has the cards, another pulls an imaginary deck out of his pocket, shuffles it, deals imaginary hands all round. The players pick up their phantom hands, sort them out in thin air. 'We had just got round to bidding,' Miller later was to recall, 'when the guy decides his eye is all right.' Botham, meanwhile chatting with Palmer, makes a prediction. 'I'll get him on the next ball,' he says. 'it never fails after a hold-up like this.' Botham now has set a challenge for himself: get Sharma, first ball. He thunders in, lets go a good ball, just short of a length. It pitches on the dreaded ridge, holds up, lifts. Sharma, unsettled after the long delay, gets a thick nick – straight back to Taylor. Botham leaps, twirls, charges down the wicket in glee and his mates swarm round him. Botham: 98 Test wickets. India: 96 for seven.

Botham's profuse wicket-taking has sent a palpable chill through the India changing-room. The observant Gaekwad recognises the growing pessimism brought on by Botham's inexorable tumble of wickets. 'Ian was getting bigger and bigger in our minds,' Gaekwad says later, 'some people who were still to bat didn't want to watch him bowl. They left the balcony or turned away from the television set.' The faint-hearted Indians had little time to avoid seeing the pillage. Bharat Reddy, the wicket-keeper, lasts eight balls and goes without scoring, out plumb lbw to a well-pitched-up ball from Botham. Botham: 99 Test wickets. India: 96 for eight.

Plumb. Wicket No. 99 is that of India's wicket-keeper Bharat Reddy, lbw, for 0.

India are in rout, their defences collapsed. With two wickets standing and three weak batsmen to defend them, the England attack is eager to get among them. No bowler is more eager than Botham: one more wicket and that nagging 100th Test wicket will be his. In the slips for Lever, he fears the next two wickets will fall before he gets his hands on the ball to bowl again. He laughs to himself: maybe Lever will listen to reason. Botham signals, spreading his arms wide, telling Lever to bowl wide. Lever shakes his head and grins. India survive two Lever deliveries but the third one is bunted down towards cover point by Venkat. The non-striking batsman, Karsan Ghavri, the best of the remaining India batsmen, senses a run and regaining strike. He shouts for a run and sets off down the wicket. Gower swoops in on the dribbling ball, snatches it up in one fluid motion and shatters the one stump that is visible to him: 96 for nine.

The spinner Bedi comes in, chin up, *patka* held high. His swinging swagger belies the fact that he is among the poorest batsmen in Test cricket. His Test average, about 9·5, is inflated beyond his talent, for he goes in last and sometimes the Indian innings dies at the other end. To bowlers, Bedi is a sure wicket, a knock-over, Marilyn Monroe drugged. Botham again implores Lever to bowl wide to Bedi. He won't. Bedi lasts two minutes – exactly four balls – before being clean-bowled by Lever. India: 96 and all out.

Lever makes a poor show of contrition as England come off the field. 'Sorry, Both,' he says. 'You'll have to wait until next digs.' With only eighty minutes until stumps, Botham is aware that his work is done for the day. But it has been a good day, by any Test standards: 19–9–35–5. As he walks through the pavilion, his father, come from the guests' 'Q' stand, walks over to him. 'Bad luck,' his father says, consolingly, 'but never mind.' Botham climbs the flight of stairs and, as England go out and make 53 runs for the loss of a wicket, he sits by himself in the changing-room. A feeling of melancholia sweeps over him, followed soon by a rising sense of anger. Five wickets. *Five wickets!* He curses. 'I've just got five bloody wickets in a Test innings, and people are disappointed,' he says to himself. 'This record thing is getting to everybody. And it's beginning to get to me.'

FOUR

The Battle with Gavaskar

A deluge of rain, the heaviest groundsman Fairbrother had seen in his many years at Lord's, fell during the following day. The ground staff did heroic work, swiftly covering the square and pushing a glaze of water into a lake at the Tavern side of the ground. A fan plunged into the lake but, otherwise, there was little to cheer about: in forty minutes of play 51 balls were bowled and as Botham clumped round the changing-room in his batting pads, England ended the day on 72 for three wickets. Fairbrother's miracle-workers had saved the match, however, and the Test resumed on the third day. It was Saturday and Botham, neither bowling nor receiving a ball on the previous day, was in the news. His regular column, ghost-written by Ian Jarrett, appeared in the *Sun*. It is a superior pop column and this week it discussed the England team in the changing-room. Bob Willis was forbidden to watch England bat for, once he set foot on the balcony, a wicket would fall. Graham Gooch was a spot-on mimic, especially of Geoff Boycott. Botham, with Jarrett, also wrote of Derek Randall. 'The public have come to know Derek Randall as "Arkle", because of his speed,' they said, 'but in the England dressing-room we call him "Accident" because he breaks up more things than a scrap-merchant.'

Randall and Botham, in fact, were involved in an accident while batting together that afternoon. Botham came in at 185 for four, with Randall at the other end, and stepped up the scoring rate under the threatening rain. They were in full throttle together when Randall played a ball towards mid-on. Shout and counter-shout were lost in a tangle of confusion and Randall was easily run out. It was a stupid blunder. The England changing-room was angry. 'Botham's running-out of people is the worst part of his batting,' Brearley was to say later. 'In that case at Lord's, it was Randall's fault as much as Botham's but if Botham had been alert to the situation he could have stopped the run-out. He can be selfish. He can get so carried away with his own performance that all he thinks about is getting at the bowlers.' Botham was to brood over the wanton run-out but equally over the manner of his own dismissal soon after it. He was settled in, looking to a fast and big innings when, on 36, his concentration lapsed. In a trice he was trapped awkwardly, half-forward, and bowled by the spinner Venkat. Botham was furious. He stalked off, beating the air and his pad with his bat. Still, at close of play, England were cruising into calm waters: 357 for seven wickets, a lead of 261 runs.

Given good weather and a flurry of runs before Brearley declared, it appeared that

England were on course for their second Test victory of the series with India. Given, too, that Botham and the other England bowlers could once again sweep away the cream of the India batsmen, Vengsarkar, Viswanath and, finest of them all, Gavaskar.

Gavaskar, at 30, already numbers among history's handful of Indian cricketers. His reputation extends beyond all boundaries, though, for Sir Donald Bradman, no spendthrift of praise, regards Gavaskar as the finest contemporary opening Test bat in the world, and by the end of the series Sir Leonard Hutton, writing in the *Observer*, was to speak even more highly of the Indian. 'He has the skill, patience and stamina,' said Sir Leonard, 'to become the greatest record-breaking Test batsman of all time.' High praise indeed, but praise not lightly offered. Gavaskar's batting average for the four-match England series was to be 77·43 runs, a figure not inflated by a single not-out, and his high score of 221 later at the Oval was to suggest a record almost too breathtaking to mention. The 221 was his 20th Test century, a total which equalled that of Ken Barrington and trailed only Neil Harvey (21), Colin Cowdrey and Wally Hammond (22), and Garfield Sobers (26), and left him within range of Bradman himself who scored 29 centuries in his Test career. His 221 also was the highest double-century ever scored by an Indian against England, surpassing the 203 achieved in 1964 at Delhi by the Nawab of Pataudi.

It is no wonder then that Gavaskar is regarded with deference by his team-mates as he prepares to bat in the India changing-room. His batting preparations, repeated so regularly over the years, now assume the air of ritual. In the warmer cricketing climates, they take about fifteen minutes; in England, where the weather is coldish, about five minutes longer. If Gavaskar is to go in at the beginning of a day, they follow this form: first he jogs in place, soundlessly, on the balls of his boots. He stands only 5 ft 5 ins, a neat, tight figure with a happy, round, cherubic face. As he jogs, the toes of his boots appear to curl up, like those of a story-book pixie, for his boots are too long for his feet. His feet are size 7, his boots size $7\frac{1}{2}$, because his feet are unusually broad and to accommodate this width he needs a longer boot. After jogging five minutes, Gavaskar takes up his bat and plays imaginary shots, straight and correct, off the front foot then elegantly off the back.

The little Indian then stops and slips his box down his trousers. 'The moment I slip on my box I stop talking with people,' he says. His voice is cheerful, crisp, educated and decorated with something near to Welsh rhythms. 'People stop talking to me. Nobody asks me to sign an autograph sheet. Nobody asks me if I want coffee. Nobody wishes me good luck. Nothing. I am left alone.' Gavaskar then plays a few more phantom shots, straight down the line and defensive, and sits on a bench. He puts on his pads. On his left forearm, he straps on his arm guard, a long pad he has been wearing since India's 1976 tour of the West Indies where such fast bowlers as Roberts and Holding beat a fearful tattoo on his forearm.

Gavaskar shakes out his floppy white sun hat. He cherishes the hat. It is a present from Zaheer Abbas, the Pakistan and Gloucestershire player, given on the occasion of the resumption of cricketing relations between Pakistan and India in the early winter of 1978. His team-mates felt at the time he would tempt bad luck if he wore it. 'They didn't think I would dare put it on until I had tried it out, tested its luck, in a first-class match at home,' says Gavaskar. He flouted fate, however, and first time on he scored two centuries in the Karachi match and now is seldom without it when the sun is shining.

Sunil Gavaskar

Gavaskar is sitting quietly when, at 11.25, someone switches on the television for BBC's coverage of the Test. The theme music, a bouncy tune accompanied by pictures of the series, including Botham taking a wicket and twirling in the air with delight, sets many players shuffling about and tapping their feet. The sole Sikh, Bishen Bedi, is either washing out or wrapping on a colourful *patka*. Gavaskar sits. From his neck dangle two religious medallions. One, given him by an old lady in Bombay, is an oval miniature of Krishna, a foremost Hindu deity, a god of both destruction and love. It hangs from a golden chain given him by his mother upon his return in 1971 from his spectacular debut in Test circket in the West Indies. It was a tour on which, among other wonderful batting achievements, Gavaskar scored a century and a double-century in a single Test. 'My mother is probably more ambitious for me in Test cricket than my father,' says Gavaskar. 'She wants me not only to score 100 but to keep going after that. She wants me to keep my head down and concentrate.' Such injunctions are not peculiar to his mother's family; her brother, Gavaskar's uncle, is Madhav Mantri, the former Indian wicket-keeper, and *his* injunction to his nephew has always been: 'Bowlers don't do you any favours. Don't throw your wicket away.'

The other medallion, hanging on a smooth leather thong, is a silvery one depicting one Sai Baba. Sai Baba is a controversial present-day figure in India and is looked upon variously as a fraud, a magician or a man of God. Gavaskar sees him as a man of God. 'My family believes in Sai Baba. Just before I came on this tour of England,' he says, 'I met Sai Baba. For me, he waved his hand and picked this medallion out of thin air.' Of the authenticity of this miracle, Gavaskar has no doubts.

Gavaskar is Hindu. Apart from the ebullient Sikh Bedi, so are the others in the current team. They are of the educated, privileged class. Gavaskar's father is a sales executive of a cotton textiles firm and Gavaskar, a graduate of the University of Bombay in economics and political science, is in public relations for a synthetic fibre and chemical firm in Bombay. In the way of the Anglophile Indian, Gavaskar has acquired an English nickname: 'Sunny'.

Gavaskar's wife Marshniel is on tour with him while their three-year-old son Rohan (named after the great West Indian batsman Rohan Kanhai) is with relatives at home. Little Rohan is crazy over cricket and Gavaskar is amused by the boy's pessimistic, misplaced loyalty in regard to the practice of cricketer-worship. In one particular fantasy, the Australian pace-bowler Jeff Thomson is the boy's hero, while Gavaskar is the hero's victim. Rohan refers to Thomson as 'Thommo' and stomps round practice sessions at a Bombay cricket ground chattering like a radio announcer. 'Thommo comes in and bowls to Gavaskar. Gavaskar hooks – and is caught,' he will say, then repeat over and over, 'Thommo comes in and bowls to Gavaskar. Gavaskar hooks – and is caught.' Gavaskar chuckles at the memory and adds, 'Who the fieldsman is, I don't know, but I never get dropped.'

It is Monday now, August 6, the fourth day of the Second Test. At Lord's, Gavaskar's dressing-room routine is slightly altered and shortened because earlier in the day India have been in the field. England, declaring their first innings 323 runs ahead of India at 419, have sent the Indians in for their second innings at 12.28 p.m. It is warm and sunny and Gavaskar wears his sun hat. He examines the wicket and finds it a beautiful batting strip, substantially unchanged from the first innings. He assumes his place and takes guard from umpire Palmer. 'I would like leg stump, please,' he calls. 'Yes, that is leg stump,' replies Palmer, eyeing down the wicket, thinking: all great batsmen seem to take leg stump. Gavaskar looks up again. What he sees this time stabs him with a sense of foreboding. He finds himself facing Botham or, as he later is to put it: 'Mike had given Ian the ball.' What passes through his mind at that moment is remarkable. 'Oh God, not Ian,' he says to himself. 'Not the first over, not the first ball. He is going to get me out. I am going to be his 100th Test victim.' Gavaskar's round face turns solemn. He dabs down the toe of his bat and summons his fraying resolve. 'At least I must not make it easy for Ian,' he vows, 'at least I must survive the initial overs.'

In passing it is interesting, perhaps revealing, to note that in recollecting the moment Gavaskar uses the affectionate Christian names of his opponents — 'Ian' and 'Mike'. Indians tend to do this, perhaps inspired by a sense of the camaraderie of cricket. England cricketers are inclined to take or impose upon themselves a more combative, depersonalised view of their rivals. For instance, Botham will say: 'The Indians seem like nice, gentle guys. I would like to get to know them off the field. But when I'm bowling against them, they've got the bat and I've got the ball and I'm going to get them out. It's odd, but as soon as I feel the ball in my hand I think that way. You've got to motivate yourself some way when you're bowling.'

Gavaskar later reflected on his premonition of getting out to Botham. First, he said, Botham's impending record was implanted in his mind. It was much talked about in the newspapers and on television and radio and, what is more, he had witnessed the air of fatalism in the first innings, when the Indian batsmen left the balcony, walked away from the television set, rather than watch Botham's ravage of wickets.

Gavaskar's premonition is not outside the nature of his Hinduism. 'A feeling of fatalism is within me,' he later explained, framing it in cricketing terms. 'Throughout my career I have had these little premonitions of getting out – and when they come they have always proved accurate.' He cited two Test examples. In 1974, in the England v. India Test at Edgbaston, India won the toss and batted. Gavaskar opened. 'As I walked in I had a premonition that I was going – first ball, to Geoff Arnold. I wasn't thinking of Arnold. I was thinking of *zero*, first ball, and that is exactly what happened. Caught behind by Alan Knott.' In 1978, India v. West Indies at Bangalore, the same thing happened. 'As I walked in to bat, I thought "I'm going to get out to zero," and the premonition was fulfilled. First ball from Sylvester Clarke, caught at gully.' As Gavaskar speaks, he fingers a medallion.

And as he faces Botham at Lord's this day, the Gavaskar connoisseur, of which there are millions, might have noticed something different in the stance of the little Indian. He stands more erect, marginally less tipped over towards the off stump. The reason for this is notably simple: since the Edgbaston Test, three weeks earlier, he has been using a bat whose blade is one inch longer than his usual bat. The overall length of the new bat is also greater; therefore, to avoid stubbing the toe of the blade he is forced to stand taller. Gavaskar fell upon this idea in the Edgbaston changing-room. At random, he picked up bats until he hefted one belonging to the tall all-rounder Mohinder Amarnath. Taking guard, he noticed that his body was perforce more erect. 'I recognised that with my old bat my eyes had been way outside the off stump,' he later was to recall, 'I had tended to play balls that were wide-ish. With Mohinder's longer bat I was more upright. I knew where I was. I felt I could judge balls better outside the off stump.'

The idea grew. He became excited. A week later, while the Indians were playing Gloucestershire at Bristol, Gavaskar suddenly commandeered the team bus and journeyed up the motorway to the Worcester factory of his batmaker Duncan Fearnley, the former Worcestershire opener. Together, they began shaping a bat which, a fortnight later, Gavaskar was to confidently carry, cold, into the Test at Lord's.

England have a party policy for bowling at Gavaskar. At the team dinner before the Edgbaston Test they decided he was predominantly an off-side player and therefore might be more vulnerable to balls of a good line and length outside the off stump. Brilliant as he was, the players felt that the Indian sometimes did silly things, such as to flash at a ball he might better let go. The seamers, the needle-sharp Hendrick in particular, suggested Gavaskar might fall to a 'trap' ball – that is, to a wide ball following several tight deliveries. In the series so far, their notions had come true: in the first innings of the Edgbaston Test he had been run out and in the second innings, when he looked settled in, he had been out playing at a bad ball outside the off stump from

Hendrick, a trap ball that had gone a little wrong. In the first innings at Lord's, Gooch got him out, as he flailed outside the off stump, caught at the wicket.

Gavaskar is too good a batsman to play to type, however, and on that morning Botham toyed with the idea that perhaps the Indian might fall to an in-swinger. At Edgbaston he had nearly got the Indian out by surprising him with in-swingers that nipped back off the wicket. Botham has much esteem for Gavaskar but feels dominant over the Indian. 'I never have got him out,' he thinks, 'but, on the other hand, I wouldn't say he feels comfortable facing me.'

Botham, although he has taken four first innings wickets from the Pavilion End, is happy again to start at the Nursery End. Partly, it is because on this particular day the wind is ideal: it comes into his face down the pitch, slightly right to left, which will help his swing and, being a light wind, not upset his rhythms. In fact, the massive Botham can handle a head wind better than any England pace bowler, much better, for example, than Willis, the other strong man, who in fact was not in the side at Lord's. 'A stiff wind blocks my run-up,' Willis will say, 'because my action is open-chested.' All this and the thought, always comforting, that Hendrick would be opening from the other end puts Botham in a good frame of mind.

On the field, Brearley tosses the new ball to Botham. 'Go ahead,' he says, 'You have a try. See if it swings.' Botham is the principal swing bowler in the side and Hendrick, like Botham's opening partner Joel Garner at Somerset, would rather open with a ball that is one over old, not only to see how it behaves in the atmosphere but to allow it to become slightly scuffed and easier to grip. This suits Botham, and besides, he wants the ball in his hand; he wants to get into the action quickly. Botham walks back, turns beyond his mark and comes in. Gavaskar, small as he is, smaller still at the distance of some thirty yards, always looks an impressive figure to Botham. The Indian is alleged to concentrate as profoundly as Boycott and it shows. He stands stock-still at the crease: no shuffling, no toe-tapping, no nervous bumping or lifting of the bat, just a nestled-down batsman, a picture of balance and composure.

The first ball isn't ambitious, just a loosener; Botham's looseners aren't much good but much better than they were in the past. 'They used to be awful – usually a half-volley or a long hop delivered at half pace – and worth four runs,' he admits, 'but now I've got the speed up to about three-quarter pace.' That first ball turns out to be of a good length, slowish, and well outside the off stump. Gavaskar watches it closely and rides it out; he is in no hurry. The second ball is Botham's stock ball, the out-swinger which makes up perhaps seventy per cent of his deliveries. Botham frowns; the ball has not moved much, either in the air or off the pitch. It is time to get to work and, experimenting even this early in his opening spell, Botham decides as he begins his next run to bowl an in-swinger.

Cricket balls are said to move through the air away from their shiny sides and, in sunny weather, batsmen often see, or attempt to see, an oncoming in-swinger before it leaves a bowler's hand. 'Sometimes I make an obvious show of the shiny side, hold it up for the batsman, as though I'm going to bowl an in-swinger,' says Botham. 'but as I come in I change it round and bowl an outer.' His keeper Taylor thinks this ploy is nonsense and a waste of time. Taylor also does not think batsmen look for a shine; rather, the alert ones foresee an in-swinger by noticing the position of a bowler's body. In Ian's case, Taylor has observed, the arm will come over and swing down close to his side. Taylor, however, gives full marks for Botham's outrageous attempts to deceive a batsman by offering and then not delivering an in-swinger; that's what's marvellous about Ian, thinks Taylor, he'll try *anything*.

As for Gavaskar, mindful of his misadventures against Botham's in-swingers at Edgbaston, he is especially alert to such wiles, such balls. 'Ian can con any batsman who watches his run-up too closely,' he says, 'but he won't so easily fool one who waits until a ball is actually delivered and sees which way it is going. You see, if you look for the shine on a ball, you'll have preconceived ideas of what it might do. No, you can't face Ian with an idea – because he can make the ball do exactly the opposite. And he does, often.'

The ball in question swings in, not much, but Gavaskar follows it and edges it harmlessly into his pad. Botham, not yet reaching his top speed, goes on to bowl a maiden over to Gavaskar; indeed the Indian fails to score off the first nine balls he receives during Botham's spell of four overs, although, during this time, he gets off the mark with a boundary through mid-wicket off Hendrick. Botham is growing nettled: he isn't getting his line right, the ball isn't moving, the wicket isn't juicy enough, too many balls are passing untasted, wide of the off stump. Worse, he can't find that elusive rhythm which makes things happen. He tells himself: 'Get sorted out.'

Frustrated, seeking something *positive* to say with the ball, Botham's tenth delivery to Gavaskar turns out to be a bouncer. 'I'm always looking for a wicket with a bouncer,' he says. As he comes in, his wicket-keeper notices a hostile bounce in his stride. Right, thinks Taylor, Ian's going to let him have it. Botham later explains it this way: 'I don't know what happened. Suddenly, I thought I'd have a go.' There are bouncers and bouncers, of course, and the normal bouncer may rear sharply and viciously but, bowling at such a short batsman as Gavaskar, one will customarily sail harmlessly over his head. Botham therefore lets go with a less-steeply rising short-pitched ball. It is aimed, not some six feet short of halfway down the wicket, as Botham will do to the average-sized batsman, but about six feet into Gavaskar's half. The ball lifts toward the Indian's throat. Gavaskar, not perturbed, hooks at it and catches a top edge. The ball drops on one bounce to Boycott at long leg for a single run.

The duel between the great Indian bat and the irrepressible Botham is on, watched by an estimated two million BBC viewers. Among them is Sir Leonard Hutton at his home in Kingston upon Thames. The sight of Botham brings Keith Miller to his mind. They are naturally comparable; each is the complete all-rounder: hostile and resourceful bowler, adventurous bat and big cat of a slip-fielder. Sir Leonard feels that Botham, at 23, is already as good a bat as Miller but, as he watches the young Englishman on television, he thinks that Botham is not quite the bowler. Miller, in Sir Leonard's view, had better body action. 'When he released the ball he was sideways to the batsman,' says Sir Leonard; 'that gave him direction and enabled him to move the ball away off the pitch. Ian moves it, but it seems only in the air. He opens his left side a little early. He brings it round towards cover point or extra cover much earlier than Miller did.' Sir Leonard ponders Botham's problem and at last, careful not to offend, he adds, 'I've been wondering if Ian isn't a little thick round the waist. I think this makes it difficult for him to get the rotation. It wouldn't do him any harm to lose a little weight.'

Also watching, live, sitting with other players' guests in 'Q' stand at Lord's were Ian's family: his wife and two infant children, his parents, little brother Graeme, and their guest Spanish boy, Ina, up that morning from Yeovil, as well as his in-laws, down from Yorkshire. They had all come to witness Ian's 100th wicket, a happy moment

Keith Miller, the Australian, an aggressive all-rounder. Many authorities, such as Sir Leonard Hutton, were quick to see shades of Miller in the young Botham.

that had been denied them in the first innings of the match. Little Liam is growing bored and the baby, Sarah, is beginning to squirm.

Hendrick is now bowling. In the slips, Botham and Brearley discuss the problems Botham is having from the Nursery End: the ball isn't swinging for him, Botham says, nothing is *happening*. He seems to be bowling into a dead wicket. Perhaps he is trying too hard. Perhaps Lever, bowling left arm over the wicket, would find that little bit of ridge bowling from the Nursery End. Botham, after all, had taken four wickets from the Pavilion End in the first innings and, at that very moment, Hendrick is getting the ball to bounce and come through from that end. It is decided that Botham will bowl his next spell from the Pavilion End.

In the duration of the next five overs Botham stays at slip for Hendrick and Lever. He listens to Gavaskar mutter to himself, 'Concentrate, concentrate,' and realises afresh that the Indian is human, vulnerable. Gavaskar may be a master batsman but Botham has no interest whatsoever in picking up technical pointers from him. 'Once you try to emulate a great batsman,' he feels, 'you'll get yourself into all kinds of trouble.'

Gavaskar, for his part, now is in no kind of trouble whatsoever; he sends three more fours streaking to the boundary off Lever to elevate his score to 32 and India's to 50. He has now struck seven fours in about as many overs and Randall, at square-cover, has a curious, exalted feeling: Gavaskar isn't playing his best, thinks Randall whose mind, like his body, is always jumping about. Gavaskar normally wears down a bowler first, then he looks for the big score and here he is, at the crease about 45 minutes and already he's 32. The Indian is playing out of character, Randall concludes, he is peaking too early for his own good.

Oddly, Gavaskar shares the feeling. 'Derek was right', he was to say later, 'it was true. I was playing too many shots. Why? I can't understand myself because I knew it was wrong. I think the answer is that I've been among the runs on this tour. I was full of confidence and when you are full of confidence you are set for any shot. No, I wasn't content to build the slow, patient innings that India needed.'

At 1.20, only ten minutes before lunch, Botham replaces Hendrick at the Pavilion End and in his two overs he bowls all twelve balls at Gavaskar. Gavaskar edges the third ball through slips for two. Botham tries another bouncer. Gavaskar does not rise to it. It is three minutes before lunch and, in his last over, Botham tries to rip up any roots of anxiety that Gavaskar might be suffering through these last moments. He experiments erratically, searching for a last key, a last door to a wicket. He tries using the entire width of the crease, veering left or right at the last moment before his delivery to explore, explode a sudden angle on the Indian. Gavaskar is not ruffled, but to say he is ready for this sort of oblique, flanking attack is not altogether true. The Indian recognises this as one of the finest weapons in Botham's armoury. 'I can't think of a bowler in the world who uses the crease as much as Ian does,' he will say (and England keeper Taylor will agree). 'When he runs in at you, you have no indication which way he will swerve – if he swerves at all. He doesn't observe the norms of a seam bowler. When a seam bowler goes wide of the crease, you can normally expect an in-swinger, but from out there Ian is just as likely to bowl an out-swinger.'

The story of Botham's command of the crease is a cameo in the study of the remarkable man. It began in 1977, a few weeks before his Test debut at Nottingham. 'One day I was messing around in the nets at Taunton, looking at the crease, and I got thinking about angles,' he recalls. 'I started bowling all sorts of rubbish, near to the stumps and wide of the crease, and I said to the Somerset blokes, "How does it feel?" They said they didn't notice.' Botham blazes at the memory of his action making no imprint. Yet in the county match, against Northamptonshire at Weston-super-Mare, which directly followed Botham's first Test, he began experimenting outrageously and took three wickets by bowling out-swingers from wide of the crease. 'As soon as he

41

became an England player,' says Somerset's veteran wicket-keeper Derek Taylor, 'he had the confidence to experiment more and more.' Against Gavaskar, Botham now finds no satisfaction in this probing, experimental pattern, and at lunch India are 52 without loss. Gavaskar is 34, only one of the runs off Botham, whose figures are 6–2–14–0 – respectable figures but in one respect deficient for such a wicket glutton.

At lunch, Botham takes off his boots in the changing-room, pulls off his soaking-wet shirt, drinks a glass of orange squash and sits resting, smoking a cigarette. He takes only a bit of lunch: three slices of beef, ice-cream and several cups of tea, heaped with sugar. In 42 minutes, in a clean shirt, he is bowling again, from the Pavilion End for a spell of four overs. Bowling mostly at Chauhan, it is a probing and tidy spell, with one maiden, yet a spell unrewarded by a wicket. Eight overs later, Edmonds breaks the Indian stand at 79 when he has Chauhan caught off bat and pad. It is shortly after this – Hendrick nearing the end of his spell and Botham due to return – when his fellow slips begin to provoke him. It is signalled by a two-handed pot-stirring gesture from captain Brearley.

'For Heaven's sake, you Gorilla,' says Taylor, as though on cue, 'let's see some aggression this time.' Brearley adds, 'Come on, Guy, where is all this fire we hear about?' Gooch waves a verbal red rag by calling to mind something that was written during the Ashes tour of Australia by the legendary Bill O'Reilly. 'O'Reilly was right, Botham, you're no threat to anybody.' Botham's prime *provocateur* is Willis, who is not playing in this match. 'To get that little extra out of Guy, you've got to insult him,' says Willis. 'You know, "My mother bowls quicker than that", and *woosh*, next ball he's made the vital breakthrough.' In 'Q' stand, Kathy Botham, having forgotten little Sarah's baby food, has left to shop outside the ground.

At 3.20 Botham is bowling his eleventh over of the day. India is on 89, Gavaskar 49 and Vengsarkar, the new batsman, 6. Botham's first ball, as orthodox as he ever is likely to bowl, is an out-swinger, delivered from his most common delivery point, tight to the stumps. The ball drifts just wide of Gavaskar's off stump and the Indian, with dainty footwork, forward then back, gets swiftly balanced and sends the ball rifling through backward of square, more a drive than a cut. Randall can merely wave a hand at the ball as it shoots past, shoulder-high it races to the boundary. Gavaskar has reached his half-century: 53 runs. 'Well batted,' says Taylor.

The crowd breaks into generous applause, for it is the Indian's third half-century in his four innings of the series. He is surprised at the burst of acclaim. He genuinely has not known that he was at the brink of his 50, nor even that the Indian score stood at 93. While batting, Gavaskar studiously avoids looking at the scoreboard (many batsmen claim this discipline, few achieve it) or even at the clock and, in fact, he often is surprised when the umpires say it is time for tea. 'If you know how many runs you have,' he says, 'you will go into a shell and not play naturally.' His batting partners, what is more, have learned never to apprise him of scores. Gavaskar says: 'My total occupation is to deal with the bowlers who are trying to get me out.'

Three balls later Gavaskar adds a single off Botham and then, facing Edmonds bowling over the wicket, the Indian puts on five more runs to reach 59 and bring India to 99. Gavaskar is feeling in command, moving into his single purple patch since lunch. As Botham begins his twelfth over of the day, at 3.27, Gavaskar has retained the strike. It is to be a tumultuous over.

First ball of the over and a sense of impending drama has seeped over the field.

Randall mills around, looking like a deep-sea diver in his crash helmet, feeling that something is bound to happen. Botham is eager at the thought of bowling to the Indian. 'The runs are coming for him,' he thinks, 'and that suits me fine.' A rapport, peculiar to sport, has grown up between bowler and batsman. Botham recalls the moment. 'When you spend a lot of time bowling at a guy, you get to understand him and like him,' he explains. 'You can see him nestling down and looking at you, trying to gee himself up, talking to himself – "Concentrate, concentrate" – and a nice feeling comes over you. It's a sort of a sixth sense: just you and him and a cricket ball.'

At the crease Gavaskar is beginning again to rise into euphoria, a giddy rhapsody of runs. He glances round the field, looking for where those runs might be had and turns his eyes to Botham only in the last thumping strides of his delivery. The ball drifts outside the off stump and Gavaskar lets it go. In the mounting tension, Botham's daughter has begun to cry in 'Q' stand. Botham's mother, growing tense herself, flops open Sarah's little stroller and together, grandmother and grandchild, they make their awkward way down behind the stand for a walk.

Second ball, Botham chooses during his run-up to bowl a slower ball. At the point of delivery, he slows down. Gavaskar reads him well. 'Ian's almost come to a stop,' he senses; 'it's going to be a slow ball.' Hendrick, in second slip, knows this, too, although his eyes are dutifully fixed on the top edge of Gavaskar's bat. A moment in time expands for Hendrick, longer and longer: he waits, waits, waits for the ball and, waiting forever, a flicker of fear passes through his stomach. 'That *prat*,' he whispers. 'Here comes a crap ball.' Hendrick later recalled the moment as wonderfully lucid. 'I was amused. I think I even chuckled. I thought that anything could happen but, Christ, that something was going to happen and whatever it was I was going to stand my ground.'

The Indian, expecting the ball to be well pitched up, has come forward on his front foot, eager to attack. The ball, however, is not only an obvious slow one, but it is badly bowled into the bargain. It didn't pitch up. It trundled in on a long hop so awkwardly that it tangles Gavaskar's timing. He hits it in the meat of the bat, but fractionally too soon. The ball explodes off the bat, high and to Randall's left, and the England player flings up his hand. He flaps at the ball, reflexively knocking it down. 'Squeeze it,' he curses himself, kicking the ground, 'squeeze it and you might catch the damned thing.' He throws his hand into the sky in disgust, tosses his head in his crash helmet. He swears at the new law forbidding players to hand their helmets to umpires between overs. Had he been bare-headed, he thinks, he might have taken the catch.

Given a life, Gavaskar takes no heed. He had mistimed the shot, true enough, but he had met the ball sweetly, *bang*, and he had felt a satisfying tremor pass up his arms and into his shoulders. Rehearsing, he replays the shot, exaggerating an artful flourish and absent-mindedly watches Randall retrieve the ball. The ball makes its looping way, player by player, back towards the bowler. The last to handle it, Edmonds, holds just a split-second too long and speaks slowly. 'Bad luck,' he grins, 'but you wouldn't want to get your 100th wicket with a strangle,' a strangle being a lucky ball, one on which a batsman hangs himself. Botham says, 'You're probably right,' although he is fleetingly annoyed with Edmonds for holding the ball that moment too long, ruining a rhythm. He is annoyed, too, that spinners, especially Edmonds, don't keep the ball shined for the seamers. 'With these guys,' Botham will say, 'the ball tends to come back with five or six marks on the shiny side. It galls me. I have to spend time on it before I start the next ball of the over.' Botham shines the ball firmly under his right thigh. In the slip cordon, Gooch, Hendrick, Brearley and Taylor are disappointed at the ball going down, yet they joke over the fact that there might have been a touch of luck in Botham's 100th wicket. It would be typical that such a bad ball, such a 'strangle', should bring him his 100th wicket. Botham will try *anything*, they conclude, even a crap ball. Returning to his mark, Botham's annoyance has now shifted to himself. He is annoyed that Gavaskar so obviously has 'read' his slow ball. He absolutely *must* learn that weird slow ball from Neil Hawke and include it among his weaponry.

Third ball and Botham turns and once again comes pounding in. Cradling the ball, grasping it in his right hand, he senses that it has gone a bit soft, even for its middle-aged life of 39 overs. The hell with it. Botham decides Gavaskar is ripe for a bouncer. In the back of his mind he knows that when bowling into Lord's ridge from the Pavilion End, especially today, any ball can behave unpredictably. It might stay low, it might lift. Botham veers tight to the stumps and bangs one in short.

Gavaskar's nimbleness, although he is to be beaten by the ball, will show up as a quick little three-step minuet on BBC film. Settling first on his back foot, the little Indian moves rhythmically forward as Botham's foot hits the crease. But, seeing the steep bang-down of the ball, Gavaskar moves back and finds himself overbalanced in no man's land. 'I was trying to get out of the way,' he is later to recall, 'but I had already committed myself across, so I was in line with the ball.' The ball plunges at him, shoulder-high. He fends, tries to drop his wrist. At the same time, he senses the ball will hit his bat or gloves and he relaxes the grip of both hands on his bat. 'Some batsmen relax only the bottom hand in these circumstances,' he says later, 'I relax both, so that sometimes the bat is knocked out of my hands.' By doing this he has deadened the concussion of the blow and reduced the danger of the the ball carrying to a fielder. It works. The ball skims off his glove and just fails to reach Brearley at first slip. Gavaskar is unmoved. It wasn't my mistake, he tells himself, it wasn't a genuine chance.

Gavaskar appears to the crowd, the Press Box and television viewers to be all in a tangle, at sixes and sevens with himself, but he feels in control of the situation. In fact, he later considers that after that ball he was *too* confident, carried away by this sense of safety. The England players nearer at hand feel a different sense of excitement. He's getting into a little bit of a state, thinks Brearley, Botham is getting worked up and Gavaskar is getting worked up in reply. Taylor thinks: Gavaskar's got the bit between his teeth; he is going to play a shot a ball. In the crowd, Botham's mother with little Sarah has pushed through the passageway between 'Q' stand and the pavilion. The child sits in a forest of legs while her grandmother watches the play. Kathy Botham, with the baby food, is outside Grace gate, coming in.

It was at this point, Gavaskar decided later, that he should have stepped away from the crease and gathered his wits about him. He should have paused to gather together the loose ends of his concentration. In fact, he neglected a device he usually employs under such uncertain circumstances. 'After I play a bad shot and I begin to feel my concentration going,' he explains, 'I cup my face like a horse wearing blinkers, and look straight down the wicket and say to myself, "Keep playing straight, keep playing straight."' But excitement overrode his caution: there were runs to be had.

Fourth ball and Randall later likes to recall the scene: 'Ian was so worked up you could see the foam coming out of his ears. Further, Randall remembers Botham's action: 'He started his run-up with two long, walking strides, then he bounced three or

ENGLAND v. INDIA at Lord's, London — 2nd TEST — 6.8.79

INDIA — 2nd INNINGS

BOWLERS (H.D.BIRD) (K.E.PALMER)

4th DAY TIME	PAVILION END BOWLER	O.	NURSERY END BOWLER	O.
3:20	BOTHAM	11		
23			EDMONDS	12
27	" (over wkt.)	12		

BATSMEN

SCOREBOARD LEFT SCORING	BALLS	6s/4s	SCOREBOARD RIGHT SCORING	BALLS	6s/4s
GAVASKAR 102	7		VENSARKAR 21		–
2L 6 / 4..1	106	8	..		23
9 7 / 2....3	112				
3●6 X E / ....W	117	8			23	–

NOTES

M16 NB1
GAVASKAR'S 50:132'
• Dropped cover (Randall) — hard hit sq.cut
Short of 1st slip
BOTHAM'S 100th WKT

END-OF-OVER TOTALS

O.	RUNS	W.	'L' BAT	'R' BAT	EXTRAS
37	89	1	49	6	3
38	94		54		
39	99		59		
39⁵	99	2	59	6	3

Botham's 100th wicket, as recorded on Bill Frindall's scorecard. Notice Frindall's record of the balls of the over from Botham and consult key on p. 80.

four strides. When he does that, his blood is up.' It is difficult for the onlooker to detect these bounces, especially looking down the wicket, and Botham refines Randall's observations: 'I wasn't angry but I was getting keen. I was *trying*. I could see I was in with a chance. If I kept plugging away, things could happen.' Plugging away, Botham heaves one in, letting loose with an enormous grunt. The ball is short and lifts just outside the off stump. Gavaskar just fails to get a touch and is beaten.

Fifth ball, Botham thunders in and, in the last two strides, impulsively swerves off, wide of the crease, trying to start the ball angling in towards the batsman. By bowling wide of the crease, he is forcing the impression upon the batsman that he must play the ball. The ball slams off the wicket, short of a length, and races wide of the batsman. Gavaskar misreads the bounce and shifts onto his back foot. He tries a clumsy cover drive but the ball stays low and ticks the bat – 'Just kisses the bottom edge', is the way Gavaskar is to remember it – and this time carries ankle-high to Brearley who makes a tumbling catch, one-handed, left-handed.

It happened! Botham, swerving back and sprinting down the wicket, bursts unaware past Gavaskar's hand of congratulation and heads straight towards Brearley and the caught ball. In the passageway beside 'Q' stand his mother turns and begins thumping on the collarbones of the woman beside her. 'He's done it! He's done it!' she shouts, then gasps as she sees the woman she is thumping is a police woman. 'Oh God,' she thinks a moment later, 'I can see the newspaper headlines tomorrow morning: "Botham gets 100th wicket. His mother jailed."' Kathy, at the gate, hears the uproar. The gateman, recognising her, says, 'Your husband's got it!' Kathryn, thrilled, clapping, wonders, should I tell him I missed it?

In the Press Box the Indian journalist, Mihir Bose, writing for *Midday* of Bombay, is speculating over the odd sight of Gavaskar thrusting out his hand to Botham so soon after he was out. 'That gesture and the point of the story is simple: concentration,' Bose writes. 'Gavaskar had allowed Botham to lead him up the Khyber Pass and over the precipice in that over.' The journalist perhaps is hard on his countryman but, on reflection, what in fact was the role of Gavaskar's premonition in his dismissal? 'My first thought when I saw Mike take the catch was "that's Ian's 100th wicket",' he later was to say. 'Perhaps the premonition was still deep in my mind, I don't know, but as I returned to the changing-room all I could think of was how stupid I was to get out in that way.'

Botham was not to get Viswanath out, nor was England to win the match which, since rain washed out much of the second day of play, appeared doomed for a draw. Botham struggles through the rest of the day, though, and after giving a series of Press interviews, he is called out on the pavilion balcony overlooking the field to speak to BBC radio. It was shortly after that, finally free to return to the England changing-room, that he runs into Gavaskar. The Indian has been looking for him. 'I must be the last man in the ground to congratulate you,' says Gavaskar and then, smiling, he adds, 'You know, when I saw you opening the bowling I had a premonition you would get me out.'

Botham was to get no one else out that day, bad light stopping play with India on 196 for two; nor did he strike on the final day of the match. India fought doggedly and, mostly on the strength of centuries from Vengsarkar (103) and Viswanath (113), the match was drawn. Vengsarkar was made Man of the Match, Botham was celebrated by such newspaper headlines as 'Ton-up!' and 'Done It!' and already the cricket

100! The milestone Test wicket, Gavaskar caught Brearley, bowled Botham 59, at Lord's.

historians were setting Ian a new target. Botham needed 140 more runs to achieve the rare Test double of 100 wickets and 1,000 runs and, if he got them over his next three Tests, he would achieve the feat in the fewest Tests of any man in history.

Kathy Botham later tells her husband she missed the wicket.

FIVE

Up to the Test

I. The Debut Series: Good balls, Rubbish and Luck

On the evening of July 23, 1977, a Saturday, Botham was pouring down a pint of lager at the Gardeners Arms, a favourite watering hole among cricketers in Taunton. He was mildly dispirited, for he had scored only seven of Somerset's 351 championship runs against Worcestershire that day but, as though to lift these spirits, his companion Dennis Breakwell soon came through the door. 'Did you hear the news?' said Breakwell. 'Chris Old has been declared unfit. I bet you £5 you're picked to replace him.'

The challenge briefly plunged Botham into a dilemma: he is not one to bet against himself yet, equally, he is loath to be seen to back off a bet. 'You're on,' he said, 'I'll take it.' The next day Botham learned over the radio that he had lost his £5. Indeed, he had been selected to the England team to face the Australians in the Third Test the following Thursday at Nottingham. It was a milestone moment, dropped out of headlines only by the news that Boycott, after months in the wilderness, had been recalled into the England fold. It was paramount news in Somerset – 'Brilliant Botham, Toast of the Cider country' – and Botham received floods of letters, only one of which appears in his cuttings book: congratulations from his bank manager in Yeovil.

The Test and Country Cricket Board followed up the invitation by posting Botham a letter containing the 'Condition of Acceptance and Notes and Instructions for Test Matches'. It was a long and exciting document, containing sixteen clauses, one of which stated that the TCCB were to be notified immediately if he was not 'completely fit'. Another said 'the fee offered to each cricketer would be £210 (Captain £32 additional), 12th man on duty throughout the Test Match £116'. The four pages literally covered topics from head to toe. For instance, Botham would be issued with a cap, a blazer, a tie, a sleeveless sweater, and a long-sleeved sweater. While these items could be replaced, Botham was told, 'a new blazer may only be issued to a cricketer, who is still playing for England, after a minimum of eight years'. Any visible form of advertising insignia on any cricket clothing or equipment (other than bats) was forbidden when playing in any Test match. 'Pads and boots must be plain white and batting gloves, if not plain white, must be one plain colour.' As for his toes, Ian's big ones would be insured for £1,600 each, his other ones £600 each: his life, if taken while on duty, was worth £30,000. 'You are requested to report to the England captain on

48

the Test Match ground, i.e. Trent Bridge,' wrote Alec Bedser, Chairman, TCCB Selection Sub-Committee, 'not later than 3 p.m. on Wednesday, 27th July, 1977.' Driving his sporty TR7 at great speed (and at 10p a mile) towards Nottingham, Botham reflected on his recent encounters with the Australians.

At Bath, in blissful May, Somerset had beaten the tourists for the first time in history. Somerset had thumped them by seven wickets, with Botham crashing the winning boundary off the spinner Kerry O'Keeffe. It had been a typical match for the ubiquitous Botham, for not only did he take the first catch of the match but he raked out five wickets from the visitors' line-up, including those of gifted David Hookes and the former Somerset star Greg Chappell. Best of all, he scored 59 runs (including 3 sixes) in the first innings and was 39 not out at the kill.

The following week, Botham again played against the Aussies, in the MCC match at Lord's. This time he came unstuck. Botham lost his rag against the pugnacious Rodney Marsh; he tried to bounce Marsh and was hooked for four; he bounced again, and again was smartly hooked. Botham thereupon flung down the gauntlet: he foamed over into a bouncing war with Marsh – and lost it, getting smashed round the ground. Finally, captain Brearley took him off, suggesting that MCC was engaged in a cricket match not a virility test. In time Botham was to take three wickets in the match, while, at the crease, he scored a lacklustre 10 and a duck. MCC lost the game by 79 runs and Botham, for his costly temper and quiet bat, feared he had lost favour with the selectors.

In July, as Botham travelled towards Nottingham, so too did the Australians who had recently refuelled with a convincing three-day victory over Gloucestershire at Bristol. They rejoiced in the news that Botham would replace Old. They fancied getting at the wayward youngster. 'We looked on Botham not so much with disrespect as without respect,' their captain, Greg Chappell, said. 'He bowled a lot of bad balls and we reckoned we could get runs.' Further, the Bath experience had taught Chappell a lesson: Botham wasn't going to see a lot of the likes of O'Keeffe and Ray Bright; the impudent newcomer was more likely to face the firepower of Thomson, Max Walker and Len Pascoe.

Botham, for his part, did not relish beginning his Test batting career against the most hostile of Australians; in the changing-room on the morning of the first day he entertained seditious thoughts. The Trent Bridge wicket as usual had looked a good wicket, invitingly full of runs on inspection that morning, yet, sitting there, Botham had hoped Brearley would lose the toss.

Trent Bridge was packed out, because Derek Randall, the local hero, was playing; and the gates were soon to be shut. The last thing Botham wanted was to sit out the next few hours in the changing-room, brooding and watching, smoking one cigarette after another as he waited to walk on to the field – alone with his bat – and before such a crowd. As luck would have it, Brearley lost the toss. Botham relaxed, trotted onto the field. Hendrick and Willis opened the England bowling. The Australian openers McCosker and Ian Davis had taken the visitors' score into the 30s when Botham came on as first-change bowler. Brearley set him a conservative field: two slips, a gully and a third man. Botham frowned down the wicket at his captain. He wanted a more attacking field: three slips; in fact, he actually wanted *four* slips, but he didn't have the courage to ask for the fourth. He got neither and second ball McCosker edged a shot, at catchable height, straight through where third slip would have been. Botham held his tongue but, glaring accusingly at his captain, punched his hands on his hips. This was the beginning of a friendly, running dispute which, on occasion, was to flare up between Botham and Brearley throughout their mutual Test days. 'Balls going through where third slip ought to be doesn't happen very often,' says Botham, 'but it only has to happen once and I'm fuming. I'll moan and groan and sometimes Brears will agree to give me a third or a fourth slip.'

Botham toiled on. He tried one in-swinger and another and soon, as Chappell had predicted, he was scattering his deliveries: long hops, half-volleys and balls sent skidding down the leg side. It was a vital stage of the match, the opening Aussie partnership remaining unbroken and into the 50s. Between overs Brearley and the wicket-keeper Alan Knott spoke beseechingly to their brawny boy in the slip cordon: just seek a perfect line, Botham, just bowl your stock out-swingers. Botham later recalled the conversation. 'I sort of said yes,' he remembers, but, for all intents and purposes, their appeals fell on deaf young ears, for the headstrong Botham persisted in his wayward attack. The Australians responded with gratitude. 'After a while, I said to myself, "All right, come on, get a couple of maidens,"' Botham concludes, 'but by then it was too late.' The ball was taken away from him.

The England breakthrough finally came. Australia were at 79 when Davis, fooled by a short ball from Derek Underwood, popped it up. Botham took an easy catch at mid-on and was over the moon. If Underwood had taken the first wicket of the match Botham, too, had been in on the action; in his first Test he had been party to the first dismissal. With the fall of that first wicket, he stamped his hallmark on Test cricket: look for the ball and, invariably, you will find Botham.

Botham was brought back to bowl just after tea, suitably castigated. The innings hung in the balance: 131 for two. The first man to face Ian was Greg Chappell, staring down the wicket with that elegant haughtiness. Chappell felt in command. He later recalls the moment: 'Hendrick had been doing so much of the bowling, giving away nothing, tying us down, that it was becoming a very frustrating period for Hookes and myself. We were happy to see Botham.' The very first ball Botham bowled to Chappell was a loosener. The Australian saw it clearly, all the way in. 'It was a great, fat, long hop, wide of the off-stump,' Chappell recounts. 'I got so excited, thinking "Well, there's four runs," that I lost my concentration.' The ball didn't bounce as much as he expected and in trying to hit it on the up and through the covers, Chappell got an inside edge and dragged the ball onto his stumps. Chappell clamped his eyes shut in disgust. Botham, equally dumbfounded, raised a meek right arm and then, recognising his conquest, launched himself down the wicket. It was a bull charge which, in years to come, would be his signature victory salute: a low, almost crouching charge, shirt-tails loose, trousers drooping, a grin bursting across his face and both arms flung into the air. 'It was a crap ball,' he said later, 'but I'll take the wicket.' Botham had taken his first Test wicket – off one of the game's greatest batsmen.

There are few sportsmen in the world who are as much inspired by their own success as Botham. Botham's tail was up. To Knott, his pace seemed to grow faster after that wicket, more dedicated and purposeful, and best of all, his marvellous out-swingers appeared to move later and later away from the bat. Doug Walters was the next to go, blundering after a ball outside the off stump, giving Hendrick a routine slip catch. Test wicket number two.

Marsh came in. The sight of that little walrus awakened memories of the humiliation

One down and 99 to go. Ian's first Test wicket, Greg Chappell bowled for 19, taken on his first Test day, July 28, 1977 at Trent Bridge against Australia.

Marsh, first softened by a bouncer, is trapped lbw.

Botham had suffered at Lord's. He would get the beggar this time. First ball, Botham came pounding in and at the last moment a thought raced through his mind – 'The last thing he's going to expect is a bouncer' – and he bowled a bouncer, whistling it past the surprised Australian's cap. Marsh's eyes bugged. Botham glanced at his first slip where Brearley's face took on an air of both worry and pleasure. 'He was thinking of the bollocking he had given me at Lord's. Had I lost my rag again?' Botham recalls. 'He was afraid that I'd bounce him again, next ball, and get slaughtered.' Botham didn't bounce him: the first had served its unsettling purpose. Botham came back with his stock ball, an in-swinger to the left-hander, and Marsh, wrong-footed, trapped, late on the shot, was lbw. Test wicket number three.

In an amazing run of 34 balls Botham that afternoon was to take four wickets at the cost of only 13 runs and by the end of the day, bowling with beautiful rhythm and control, he added the scalp of Thomson to raise his bag to five wickets. Walker went meekly, edging to Hendrick, and Thomson had a slog at a good-length ball and was taken behind. Australia's innings, which had begun so promisingly, was reduced to rubble by the brash newcomer from Somerset. All out: 243. Botham: 20–5–74–5. The teams were later presented to the Queen and Prince Philip, on tour of the area. The Queen had missed the onslaught but, pausing before the new young England hero, she said with regal understatement: 'It looks as if you've been doing some work.' Botham, a monarchist, for once was lost for words. 'She is a woman who commands great respect,' he will say. 'England would never be the same without their Queen or King.'

Botham's inaugural Test wicket, plundered from Chappell, may have been lucky.

51

But, as Napoleon said, it is better to have lucky generals than good generals and Botham always has been a man who makes the most of his luck. He enjoyed a stroke of it two days later as England batted. Again the luck was made possible by Chappell. Botham came in with six wickets down, England at 297. Botham faced Thomson. Chappell was at first slip, a full stride closer to the action than he would have been in Australia for, he says, a ball stays lower in England. Chappell later took up the story. 'I can remember what happened next quite vividly, as though it were in slow motion,' he said. 'Botham tried to force Thommo's third ball off-side and got a thick edge. He hit a fast skimmer, straight at me. I though it was a routine catch. I would take on my left side about hip-high. But it kept rising and got awkward, and hit me on the left thumb.' The catch went down and Chappell cursed, briefly and colourfully: he would have easily taken the catch at home. Botham was given a reprieve.

Ian played and missed the following two balls. He was beaten thirteen times in 30 balls before lunch, not an auspicious debut. Still, he went on to score 25 runs in his innings. In the second innings he took no more wickets while yielding 60 runs and was not required to bat as England won the match by seven wickets. 'That's how I started my Test career,' he was to say later, 'some good balls, some rubbish and some luck – thanks to Greg Chappell.'

A fortnight later, when picked for the Fourth Test at Leeds, Botham's thoughts drifted uneasily to the first clause of the 'Conditions of Acceptance . . .' document, namely the clause requesting a player to immediately notify the Secretary of the TCCB in the event he is not 'completely fit'. Botham had stretched a point in inferring he was completely fit for, in truth, he felt a few twinges in his left foot. It had ached through the championship and John Player League matches against Northampton which had been played over the past several days at Weston-super-Mare. The foot had been X-rayed and found not to be broken and diagnosed provisionally as a strained ligament. Botham was given anti-inflammation tablets and deemed fit for the Test. Still, it hurt. Would it break down at Leeds? Botham put the question out of his head. Would England, already with two victories and a draw, win the match, the series and the Ashes? If so, what role might he play?

August 11, and Headingley, like Trent Bridge had been, was packed; this time chock-a-block with Yorkshiremen come to see Boycott grind out his 100th century. Brearley won the toss, England batted. Boycott came within a trace of carrying his bat, losing his wicket to close England's innings at tea on the second day. Of England's total of 436 runs, Boycott scored 191, Botham exactly 0. Botham had fallen the second day, clean bowled, during a purple patch of spinning from Bright. It was at moments like this that Botham could fall back on his old rationale: failing with the bat, he could redeem himself with the ball.

Sitting on the players' balcony of the pavilion that afternoon, cheering Boycott, waiting to redeem himself, Botham noticed clouds building up. The sight was encouraging. 'As soon as you see a few clouds in the sky at Headingley, you known the ball is going to do a bit.' he said later. 'As the sky clouded over the contrast in the colour of the wicket was quite remarkable. In the matter of an hour, it went from white to green.' In that hour, England went out on the field, anxious to get the ball seaming and swinging in the curious Yorkshire air. Botham began to move it prodigiously in the air. Knott marvelled at the movement Botham got that afternoon; in time Knott concluded that no one in cricket could move a ball so much, so late as young Botham.

Marsh again. Knott takes a brilliant, tumbling catch.

In all of his 94-match Test career, the cautious Knott decided only the ephemeral Australian Bob Massie in his 16-wicket demolition of England at Lord's in 1972 was able to make the ball swing so effectively late as Botham does on a good day.

Botham was on song. He pinned down Hookes, lbw, with a bewildering in-swinger and lured the luckless Walters with one that left him and, finding an edge, carried to Hendrick. On the following day he led the mop-up of Australia's middle and flapping tail, the crucial wicket once again Marsh's. The clouds were still about and, as Botham put it, 'the ball was swinging all over the place'. Fishing for another lbw, Botham soon pitched a ball well up, swinging into the left-hander. 'The damned thing swung too much,' Botham recalls, sounding like a man who had wound up the toy too tight, 'and it started going down the leg side.' Marsh went back on to his stumps and attempted to flick it along. He got a thin edge. Knott by that time had anticipated the shot, moved swiftly to his right. In a split second he was ready to twist back and take the ball in his left hand if it went through, or to dive and take it in his right if Marsh made the touch. 'You think the touch *could* happen,' Knott says, 'but not that it *will* happen.' Knott got a glove to the ball, fumbled it, tumbled and came up with a spectacular catch. Walker went next – 'nothing special about that ball,' says Botham – and with the score at 100, Botham bowled a beautiful, easy-paced ball that swung late and bowled Thomson. Hendrick bowled Pascoe for nought and with Australia's total 103, 333 runs behind England, Brearley enforced the follow-on. Botham was jubilant: for his second Test running he had taken five first-innings wickets – his figures were, to be exact, 11–3–21–5 – and Hendrick made the droll suggestion: 'Okay, bring Botham along for the first innings, but let's leave him here in the changing-room for the second.'

The joke was prophetic. Of the four visitors' wickets taken that afternoon, Botham was to take none and, worse, he felt renewed twinges in his foot. It again was thought to be a strained ligament and, on the physiotherapist's advice, Botham spent Sunday in his hotel room, foot up. On Monday he broke down. The incident looked innocent enough; he pushed out his foot to stop a ball, stepped on it and turned his ankle. Pain shot through his foot. Botham reluctantly came off, yielding his place to the 12th man, Alan Ealham, who was on the field at 4.40 when Randall made the historic catch of Marsh's skied drive. By an innings and 85 runs, England had won the match and the Ashes. At the moment of triumph, Ian was stretched out on the rubbing table next to the changing-room. He was gritting his teeth against a shot of pain-killer to the foot when the roar went up from the crowd. Botham flinched, cried out, as the hypodermic needle drove painfully into his foot.

The injury proved worse than had been feared. Botham had suffered a march fracture of the metatarsal bone, the one that links the body of his left foot to the third toe. It had been brought about by banging down on the foot when he bowled and, in all, he had bowled more than 600 overs for Somerset that summer. He was slapped into plaster and dropped from the England side that faced Australia in the closing, drawn match at the Oval. Hobbled, Botham also missed three championship matches for Somerset. Missing these, he also missed a chance of his first double in first-class cricket: 100 wickets and 1,000 runs in a season. His figures came to rest that year at 88 wickets, costing 22.53 runs each, and 738 runs, at an average 30·75 per innings.

It was a lamentable end to a glorious summer, but, nonetheless, Botham finished the year by granting cricket's most cherished and secret interview. He spoke to *Wisden*, the cricketers' almanack, who the following spring were to include him with his England team-mates, Willis and Hendrick, along with Essex's Ken McEwan and Glamorgan's Alan Jones, as one of the Five Cricketers of the Year 1977.

II. Pakistan and New Zealand: Home and Away

Botham also was named Young Cricketer of the Year 1977 by the Cricket Writers' Club and, much more important, named in the 16-man party that was to go east for a winter tour of Pakistan and New Zealand. Botham's foot was knitting. He was on a diet, taking long walks near his home in South Humberside and enjoying a short holiday with his wife and son Liam, who had been born at the end of the season. If a bitter-sweet tour, full of disappointments and successes, lay ahead, Botham was none the wiser. He looked forward to it with optimism. 'I felt I had a good chance of playing in all the matches,' he later recalled, 'but then, I always fancy my chances of playing in all my matches.'

On the barren, pancake pitches of Pakistan, though, Botham's chances looked flat from the start. It was to be a series suited to the spinners and, with Willis holding down one end in the pace attack, Old and John Lever were thought more lethal than the swing-bowling Botham. It took him only a single session in the nets at Rawalpindi, moreover, to confirm the selectors' suspicions of the unwisdom of his unbridled batting aggression. 'He tried to take on local leg-spinners and smash them out of the ground,' the captain, Brearley, later was to recall, 'and he was hopeless.'

Another problem came to a head in the following up-country match at Peshawar, the week before the First Test at Lahore. Bowling against the NW Frontier Governor's XI, Botham no-balled perhaps ten times in the first innings and, shaken by the umpires' decisions, returned to the field that evening with Old, Hendrick and his friend and Somerset captain, Brian Rose. His four team-mates stationed themselves round the

England touring party to Pakistan–New Zealand 1977–8: (front row) *Bob Taylor, Derbyshire; Mike Gatting, Middlesex; manager Ken Barrington; Geoff Boycott, Yorkshire; captain Mike Brearley, Middlesex; team physiotherapist Bernard Thomas; Derek Randall, Nottinghamshire; Geoff Cope, Yorkshire;* (back row) *Geoff Miller, Derbyshire (partly obscured); Graham Roope, Surrey; Chris Old, Yorkshire; Bob Willis, Warwickshire; Mike Hendrick, Derbyshire (partly obscured); Ian Botham, Somerset; Brian Rose, Somerset; Phil Edmonds, Middlesex; Paul Downton, Kent (obscured) and scorer Geoffrey Saulez.*

bowling crease and, kneeling down, watched Botham pound past and bowl ball after ball. At the moment of delivery they found that Botham was taking off from the ball of his front foot, which was unlike most bowlers who take off flat-footed. This, they concluded, was the source of the problem. The laws of cricket say that a delivery is to be called a no ball *if in the delivery stride, no part of the bowler's front foot is behind the popping crease, whether grounded or raised.* While Botham's foot was behind the crease, it was not grounded at the time of delivery and the England players felt that perhaps this was the reason that in the view of the Pakistan umpires he was bowling no balls. Botham decided to join this interpretation rather than fight it. He practised. He began coming down well behind the crease, a habit that has had a long-term salutary effect on his bowling: since Peshawar, Botham rarely has no-balled, either for Somerset or for England. Still, he was not called to duty in Pakistan.

Bored and frustrated, he played lots of golf and during a round at Lahore with Ken Barrington his cricket frustrations spilled over. Botham's caddy, undervaluing his player's power, took the brunt of it. Botham himself later told the story: 'We were playing this long par-5 hole and I hit an enormous tee shot – straight out to the right and into the undergrowth. My caddy, who was betting on me against Kenny's caddy, found my ball sitting up in the middle of the fairway. He told me to give it all I had: there was no way I could reach the green, which was over a hill and out of sight. I had a feeling I could reach the green, or get very close, so I took a 2-wood and hit a screamer, right up the middle. I said, "Ah, that's got to be close," and my caddy went white. Well, when we reached the top of the hill, there was this great big pond in front of the green. It had a notice saying: "Snake Infested Water – Do Not Send In Your Caddy." By which time I was furious, and pretty soon I had the guy by the scruff of the neck and was yelling: "You get in there and get that ball! I want that ball back!" He went in. After that he had a lot more respect for my distance in hitting a ball.'

In all, England drew their three Tests, won only a single first-class match in Pakistan, and lost their captain when Brearley broke his left arm, hit by a ball bowled in a match just before the final Test. Botham, apart from his one-day performances, batted only in two innings, scoring a duck and 22 not out. It is no wonder that the Somerset all-rounder led the cheering when, late in January, the plane carrying the England party lifted off from the Karachi runway, bound for New Zealand.

With its familiar food, drink and social customs, New Zealand was a breath of fresh air for Botham; he lost little time in reclaiming his Test place: a fortnight after landing, he scored a vicious and unbeaten 126 on a juicy wicket against Canterbury at Christchurch. The match, only three days before the opening Test at Wellington, was drawn but it was to be profoundly important to Botham for, apart from scoring his first century in seven months, it marked the beginning of a feud, glare for glare, bouncer for bouncer, with the New Zealand fast bowler Richard Hadlee.

Canterbury won the toss and the England XI were put in. Hadlee took the first three wickets cheaply enough, and soon Botham was gone too, bowled for a duck by the Canterbury and New Zealand veteran Bev Congdon. England were all out for 173 then turned round and dismissed Canterbury for 144, Botham taking two undistinguished wickets. In England's second innings Botham began belting the ball. Hadlee whistled in a venomous bouncer. Botham pounced, hooked it for four. Hadlee came back with another and, once again, Botham savagely hooked it. Botham backed off the crease. 'That's that!' Botham shouted down the wicket. 'Now give me another.' Hadlee pawed his jaw and gave him another and Botham again safely hooked it. The Englishman went on to make mincemeat of the pride of the New Zealand pace attack. England declared at 230 for four, all credit to Botham who was 126 not out. The first Botham-Hadlee skirmish went to Botham.

Botham rejoiced and, moving to Wellington for the First Test, rejoined his battle with Hadlee. New Zealand went in and scored 228 runs with Botham, enjoying himself, taking two wickets but regrettably not that of the resolute tailender Hadlee. England replied strongly with Boycott, now captain, grafting 77. The side slumped to 215 all out, with Botham ignominiously losing his wicket, caught in the slip cordon, to his gaunt nemesis Hadlee. The Kiwis were summarily wiped out for 123 in their second innings, two more wickets falling to the rejuvenated Botham.

Then the crunch came. England, needing only 137 to win, got away to an appalling start: Rose retired at 5 with a bruised right arm, Boycott went for 1, Miller for 4, Taylor was run out for 0, Randall fumbled uneasily towards a total of 9 runs and Roope was dismissed for a duck. 'We were in a bit of trouble,' Botham later related, with uncharacteristic understatement. 'We needed a few to win, with four wickets left, and I thought to myself, "There are two ways of playing this: either (1) try to bat for a day and a half without reaching the target, which doesn't seem logical to me; or (2) play my natural game and have a go. If the ball is there, hit it." I thought if I could get a quick 30 or 40, maybe we could end up winning this Test.' Botham had a go. 'Hadlee bounced

Fore or a six! A keen golfer, handicap 11, Botham feels playing the game does not spoil his cricket batting. Notice: tensed muscles in left forearm and open grip. Look for: banana-shaped slice.

me. I hooked him well for four. He bounced me again but this time I didn't hook it so well and it landed behind square leg, two runs. He got a little keen then, as any fast bowler would do, and sort of stared down the wicket at me. I didn't mind this at all. It was tremendous, in fact, a great sign of competitiveness and I remember shouting back at him: "Give me all you've got!" Well, he got smart. He put this bloke, Boock, back there at square leg and bounced me again. I tried to hook him and I got caught. I had taken the bait, hook, line and sinker and half the rod – and got well and truly landed – by Boock at square leg.' Botham was gone for a quick 19, England was ultimately gone for a very quick 64. The upshot was a victory, by 72 runs, that New Zealand could savour: their first triumph over England after 48 years and 48 Tests between the two countries. The ground rang out with fans serenading their heroes: 'For they are jolly good fellows', and the jolliest of them all no doubt was Hadlee, who had blown down the visitors, taking ten wickets for 100 runs. Hadlee had also won the second skirmish with Botham.

The young Englishman was spoiling for a return fight with Hadlee. It came in the Second Test at Christchurch, a fortnight after the dust was still settling over Wellington. The Test was to crackle with even more incidents than the one on the North Island and, not surprisingly, Botham was in the centre of the action. The Test began ominously. Boycott won the toss, put England in on a green wicket and within the hour he was back in the pavilion, along with Randall. 26 for two. It looked as though New Zealand, who had won their first Test against England, might now win their first series. Roope and Miller stopped the rot, but suddenly the fourth and fifth wickets had fallen at 127 and 128 and in came Botham, windmilling his bat. 'I didn't see much of Hadlee that first day,' he recalled. 'He bowled me a loosener, a short-length ball without much fire, and I stood back and pulled it for four. The next morning Hadlee was fresh and racing in. He had the man out at square leg straightaway, then he started bouncing me. As the morning progressed, the more he bounced me, trying to get me to hook. But I just stood there and smiled down the wicket at him. This got him going, geed him up a bit, and he lost his line and length. he tried to bang too many into me and all he was doing was bruising his wicket-keeper's hands, because there was no way I was going to attempt to hook him.' After surviving the Hadlee blitzkriegs, he was out to the left-arm spin of Boock, but not until he had steered England clear of the shoals and reached his maiden Test century of 103 runs. After his five hours and eleven minutes at the crease, England were 293 for seven. They were all out for 418. In the New Zealand innings, Hadlee was gone, bowled Edmonds for 1, before Botham could get at him. All out for 235, New Zealand escaped the follow-on by only 16 runs.

Boycott, looking forward to an early declaration, instructed his team to go out and 'throw the bat', get the runs flowing. Such an injunction from such a dilatory batsman amused the England players and after Rose went for 7, the scoring pace slowed. Boycott was in with Randall, the England score 47, when a deplorable incident took place. The medium-paced Ewan Chatfield, bowling at Boycott, ran up and swept off the non-striker's bails, underarm, catching Randall out of his ground. It was a surprising act, taken without due warning, but the umpire had no choice but to give Randall out. The England dressing-room seethed with rage and Botham, called in at number four to hasten the scoring rate, marched with narrow eyes onto the field. 'What Chatfield had done sickened me. It was the lowest of the low,' he recalls. Prior to the incident Botham had felt sympathy for the New Zealander who had cheated death at Auckland in 1975 when he was hit in the temple by the England bowler Peter Lever. Chatfield's heart had stopped beating for several seconds on that occasion and only the administration of heart massage and mouth-to-mouth resuscitation by Bernard Thomas saved his life.

Botham took up a position well outside the crease, his bat safely stretched back into his ground. He leaned towards Chatfield who stood setting his field. Botham glared at the New Zealander as he ran past to bowl. The unrepentant Chatfield, returning to his mark, said: 'If you leave your crease, Botham, the same thing will happen to you.' Botham fixed him with a point-blank look. 'Just remember one thing, son,' he said slowly, 'you've already been "killed" once on a cricket field.' Chatfield said nothing, aware that he might come to the crease the following day against Botham.

England soon went into a stall. Boycott came down the wicket for a chat. 'I don't know what's wrong,' he said to Botham. 'I can't seem to get the ball off the bat.' Botham nodded at his captain and replied: 'Well, don't worry about it, Fiery. I'll take care of it.' England were nearing a lead of 250 runs and in no danger of losing the Test; but if they were to win it by declaring early the next morning Botham reckoned they needed more runs. If England were to get a move on then Boycott would have to be sacrificed. He would have to be run out. Botham soon received the appropriate ball and, playing it down to the off side, called for a run. Boycott started off, hesitated, cried 'No'. Botham firmly overrode the call, shouting 'Yes', and kept moving. He was careful to draw past his captain – just as the stumps were thrown down at the batsman's end. Boycott was gone for 26. England were 67 for three and, with Botham wantonly attacking for 30 runs in 36 balls, they were able to declare with a lead of 279 the following morning.

With less than a day to bowl out the Kiwis, England set grimly to their task. Willis, bowling with hangman's pity, proceeded to take four wickets for nine runs. Botham took a spectacular diving catch, went off for repairs to a split finger, returned to take another spectacular diving catch. New Zealand, 25 for five wickets, were being kept afloat solely by Hadlee. 'When he first came in to bat, he just stood there, annoying me, and I bounced him the very first ball,' Botham later recalled. 'It was a good ball, straight at him, and he just got his glove and bat handle up in front of his face in time. He went a few different colours. Pretty soon, though, he played this characteristic shot of his, flat-batting a bouncer over the slips for four. By then I was *very* annoyed. I lost my rag. I bowled badly and he smashed me all over the ground.'

It came as cold comfort that Botham, sprinting towards square leg, finally caught Hadlee. Or that Botham, still piqued, swept through the New Zealand tail, claiming the last three wickets, including that of the cowering Chatfield. Or, in fact, it mattered not a whit that Botham had played the greatest match in his Test career: 103 runs and 30 not out, eight wickets for 111 and three dashing catches. He had failed. He had lost his cool to Hadlee and when England returned to the pavilion, 174-run victors, the players turned on him in jagged good fun. 'It sank in,' Botham admitted later. 'I think the feud I had with Richard Hadlee in New Zealand matured me more than any experience I've had in Test cricket. Since then, I've curbed myself a little. I've learnt a bit about restraint.'

The Third Test, which started three days later, was played on a batsman's paradise at Auckland. New Zealand scored 315, with Botham taking Hadlee's and four other wickets. England replied with 429, Botham smashing a swift 53. The match was doomed to be drawn. 'We played for six days,' Botham recalled later, 'but on that wicket, we could still be playing.' The Pakistan and New Zealand tour thus ended with a whimper but, playing only the last leg of it, Botham had rekindled his fire. 'New Zealand was perfect for Both,' said his fellow tourist and Somerset captain, Rose. 'He came from Pakistan, angry and frustrated, his run-up sorted out and eager to prove himself on green wickets. It was ideal. His confidence grew day by day and he was a yard quicker when he came home.'

Botham's Test record to date

Batting and Fielding

Tests	I	NO	HS	Runs	Avge.	100s	50s	Ct
5	7	1	103	237	39·50	1	1	6

Bowling

Balls	Runs	Wkts	Avge.	BB	5W/I	10W/M
1,246	513	27	19.0	5–21	4	—

The Pakistanis arrived in England in April 1978. The weather was cold and rainy and they played little cricket, only nine full days in their first six matches. A tranquil group, they devised a way to defuse their flashes of frustration. It involved a silent physical gesture that worked this way: when insulted by a team-mate, or provoked by misfortune, a player would assume an air of wounded dignity and, without saying a word, lift and turn his chin. 'I don't know who started it, it just grew,' the vice-captain, Wasim Raja, said at the time. 'Now it's become a cult joke – and a useful one, too.'

The Pakistani, turning his other cheek, is alien to Botham who likes his cricketing relationships to be friendly and bellicose. He knew few of the Pakistanis, save Wasim Raja who played league cricket in the North, and therefore could not construct a rivalry similar to the one he enjoyed with Hadlee in New Zealand or, later, with Rodney Hogg in Australia. The Pakistanis, without their Packer players Mushtaq, Asif Iqbal, Majid, Imran and Zaheer Abbas, whom Botham finds the hardest man to get out in county cricket, offered no personal challenge to the robust young Englishman.

Still, and as usual, Botham had things to say with bat and ball during the series. For instance, he took the first Pakistani wicket in the opening Test at Edgbaston. He had the graceful Mudassar Nazar, caught and bowled, for 14. 'A half-volley and he went to drive it and got over the top of it,' recalls Botham. 'Actually, I didn't think much of the catch at the time but when I saw it on television replay I thought it was great. Hard and low and down to my left and I caught it with both hands. That shows how *supple* I was.' It was to be the only wicket he took in the Test which, apart from the second touring Test in Perth against Australia when he got none, was Botham's lowest match yield in his run towards 100 Test wickets.

At the crease Botham soon restored his authority. Attacking the ball viciously, he scored his first Test century on home soil, a level 100 that, together with Clive Radley's

Hooked for six. On the way to his 100 in the 1978 Test at Edgbaston against Pakistan, Ian savages a delivery from Sikander Bakht.

106, propelled England to an eventual triumph by an innings and 57 runs. The sour note of the match came on the fourth and last morning when Iqbal Qasim, who had served Saturday evening as nightwatchman, was hit in the mouth when Bob Willis went round the wicket to attack him with a fourth savage bumper. Qasim was led off the field, bleeding profusely, and a great public discussion ensued over the morality of bouncing non-recognised or at least low-order batsmen. Botham takes a hard line over the incident. 'Qasim was in a negative mood in what is supposed to be a positive game. I saw nothing wrong with bouncing him and, in my view, the English Press acted like a lot of prats over it,' he said later. 'Look, a guy can't be in there for forty minutes, just blocking around, and expect to keep getting balls pitched up to him. As soon as Bob put in a short one, from round the wicket, he was in a mess, got hit and never scored again all through the series.'

Botham's movable feast then travelled to London where he made his first Test appearance at Lord's, the shrine of the game. This was the occasion of his entering the changing-room and, as though with some divine right, making a bee-line for Sir Leonard Hutton's sofa and taking it once and for all as his own. Botham, as he has said before, rises to the big occasion and he was to do so this time at Lord's. After it was over, after Pakistan had been dispensed with in the wet Third Test and New Zealand in their series that summer, the annual *Wisden* was to write this of the June match at Lord's: 'There had never been an all-round performance like Botham's in a Test match.'

The match was a day late in starting, due to rain, and Botham first softened Pakistan with his bat. 'When I went to the wicket they had four fielders round the bat,' he later was to recall, 'and by the end of the over they had one.' The remark suggests the nature of his aggression and, indeed, it took courage for the close Pakistanis to last that long for Ian, second ball, crashed a loose, leg-side delivery from the spinner Iqbal Qasim into the Mound stand for six. 'I went to sweep it,' he said, 'and I hit it over the top.' That brought England to 140 for five and, together with Roope, Botham swiftly saved the team from possible calamity. By the close of play he was in full cry, the tenuous Pakistan attack in shambles. 'I just went out to play and took the runs as they came,' Botham will say, but it does not escape notice that his scoring accelerated as closing time neared and, last over, he sent a ball galloping through the off side to the boundary to reach 102. It brought him his second century in a row, and his quickest at 2 hours and 40 minutes. The next day, before a crowd of 20,000, he added six more runs before dragging a ball onto his stumps. England, now safe, were all out before tea for 364.

Pakistan batted twice that day: their first innings earned them only 105 runs, Willis and Edmonds striking and spinning them aside, and they followed on. Willis quickly had Sadiq Mohammad caught behind for a duck, and then the attention turned to Botham who swept down like a wolf on the fold. By adding eight wickets to his earlier century, he set an all-round standard unmatched in Test history, a mark he himself was to break spectacularly in the Indian Jubilee Test in 1980. The first of these eight wickets fell Saturday evening, the others on Monday. They increased Botham's Test wicket harvest from 28 to 36. For the record, let Botham himself see us through the wickets:

Saturday, June 17, 1978

Wicket No. 29: Mudassar c. Taylor 10.

'The funny thing is, the ball wasn't swinging at all that evening. It was a good ball to Mudassar. I banged it in, just short of a length and it bounced a little and left him. He got an edge to Taylor.'

Monday, June 19, 1978

'The sky was bright and we thought it was going to be hard work that day. Brears put me on from the Nursery End, just to change the bowling, really. The wind was very small, coming from over by the Press Box and into my right shoulder but it was *so* small it couldn't have had a bearing on what happened. There must have been something in the atmosphere. I went up there and the very first ball swung, away it went, and everybody was surprised, not least Talat Ali, the batsman. Brearley just looked at me and said, "Carry on." '

Wicket No. 30: Talat c. Roope 40.
'It was full length, just outside the off stump and swinging away. I think the batsman read it as being a half-volley. It was on the line he thought but it continued swinging.' Talat edged the ball towards second slip where Roope was ready. Roope recalls: 'For me, this was the ideal ball and I could watch it all the way in, full-length and swinging away. I took it in one movement from my crouch, upwards and over towards my right, which is my safe side.'

Wicket No. 31: Haroon b. 4.
'That ball, without doubt, was the best ball I ever bowled to take a Test wicket. It was headed towards middle and leg and Haroon was committed to the point of no return, pushing down. Then the ball swung away incredibly late and knocked out the off stump. All I wanted to do was to bowl a simple away-swinger and look what happened.' Roope was equally impressed. 'That ball was absolutely unplayable. No one on earth could have survived it.'

Wicket No. 32: Wasim Raja c. and b. 1.
'I didn't have a mid-off and when I bowled him a big in-swinger, he went for an off-side drive and spooned it back to me.'

Wicket No. 33: Wasim Bari c. Taylor 2.
'A diabolical shot. It would have been close to a wide if he hadn't chased it.'

Wicket No. 34: Sikander c. Roope 1.
'It was a full-length ball which he tried to play defensively and got a nick.' Roope adds: 'Sikander had to play at it because the ball had been swinging so much, but he was jumpy and he pushed forward at it rather than letting it come. The ball came fairly flat to me and I just had to stay down.'

Wicket No. 35: Iqbal Qasim b. 0.
'Bob Willis, who had hit him in the mouth at Edgbaston, bowled him out in the first innings at Lord's and now he didn't have any confidence. This ball swung into him, as a left-hander, starting outside off stump and kept going down the slope. It hit middle and leg.'

Wicket No. 36: Miandad c. Gooch 22.
'With nine wickets down, the match was all over and we set a very attacking field. We put Goochy square on the off side. I bowled off stump. Straight to Gooch.'

Comparisons may be odious, but they are obvious, too, and in history only two men have twice scored centuries and taken five or more wickets in an innings: Gary Sobers did it against India in 1961–62 at Kingston (104 and 5–63) and again against England in 1966 at Headingley (174 and 5–41); Mushtaq Mohammad achieved it against New Zealand in 1972–73 at Dunedin (201 and 5–49) and again against West Indies in 1976–77 at Port of Spain (121 and 5–28). The third was Botham who had first done it

Perfect catch. Botham's 30th Test wicket, Talat caught Roope 40, provided the ideal ball for slip-fielder Graham Roope, who said: 'I took it in one movement from my crouch, upwards and over towards my right, which is my safe side.'

The best ball. Haroon bowled Botham 4. 'The best ball I ever bowled to take a Test wicket,' says Botham of his incredible in-swinger at Lord's, 1978. It took wicket No. 31.

Spooned back. Wasim Raja caught and bowled Botham 1. The fourth of Ian's eight wickets in the Pakistan innings at Lord's.

against New Zealand in 1977–78 at Christchurch (103 and 5–73). But no man had ever taken eight wickets – and Ian took them at the knock-down price of 34 runs – to add to a century. England won by an innings and 120 runs, depriving Botham of another opportunity to bat. In the anticlimactic Third Test, at Headingley, rain reduced play to ten and a half hours and in the drawn match Botham took four Pakistan wickets but was denied his hat-trick of Test centuries when he was lbw to Sarfraz for 4. Botham was named Man of the Series.

The Kiwis were in England, returning the winter visit, and once again Ian quickly took a Test wicket that is worth hearing about. It came at the Oval, first innings, with Geoff Howarth moving steadfastly towards his century. 'It was my luckiest wicket in Test cricket,' Botham will say, then rationalise his luck. 'Again, though, it was a wicket I got because I was trying something different. I came on and I bowled him a terrible ball, a rank long hop down the leg side. He could have hit it anywhere in London, so he took a long time to size it up and he hammered it. Phil Edmonds was at backward square leg and leaped and caught it one-handed. A great catch.' Howarth also remembers it. 'Sloppy ball, the worst ball in the whole series. But it fooled me. I had 94 runs on the board and here were four more. It was typical of Ian. He can bowl you four bad balls in an over and then two magic balls. This one was both.' England won the Test, Botham contributing 22 runs and three second-innings wickets and the series moved on to another of Botham's favourite grounds, Trent Bridge.

'I like it at Trent Bridge,' Botham will say, 'because it presents me with two different wickets and I can bowl two different ways.' He illustrates Nottingham's peculiar pitch characteristics by first explaining its condition when New Zealand came in late on the second day, after England had opened their account with 429 runs, 131 of them Boycott's. 'The wicket had got a little bit wet and Brears told me, "Don't try to swing it, just let it go, give it all you've got, just short of a length because the wicket is going to hop around a bit." ' Botham did what he was told. Brearley's prognosis proved correct. In New Zealand's first innings, Botham mostly sent the ball humming into the wicket and it reacted erratically, bringing him six wickets. In the last thirty minutes of the first day, he took two, on the next day four. Burgess was a characteristic victim. 'I let it go. It hopped and left him,' Botham recalls, 'and he was caught behind by Taylor.'

New Zealand's second innings was a different matter. Botham opened the day with two quick balls that achieved only a stoppage of play for bad light. The players came on again at 3.15 and after another couple of hostile deliveries Botham felt tired, perhaps fed up with doggedly following Brearley's dictum. Richard Hadlee, Botham's *bête noire*, was one of the young Englishman's victims that day, and his wicket was taken typically. Botham recounts it: 'Richard always looked for the bouncer when I bowled at him and, although it is very rare for me to bowl so many in-swingers, I gave him about four or five of them, then I pushed one across him towards the slips. He fell for it. He flashed at it and it went to Gooch.' Botham once again had done nothing with the bat, 8 runs, but once again his bowling figures were startling: 45–16–93–9. Once again, he was named Man of the Match. Once again, too, England won, this time by an innings and 119 runs.

Botham's confidence was rampant. In the Third Test at Lord's his bat was muted again, 21 runs, but when given the ball, and he was given it for 56 overs, he was crippling. He took eleven wickets that match, which was a Test record for him. The one that pleased him most, and one that reveals the pugnacious self-will of the man, came in a purple patch of three wickets for 18 in the first 8.4 overs of the second New Zealand innings. It was a turning-point of the match. The left-hander John Wright was opening the innings. 'I was trying to bowl him an in-swinging yorker,' Botham recalls. 'Twice I tried it and twice it went for four, off a full toss and a half-volley. I ran up again and tried it third ball, and bowled him. Brears was at first slip and he came up to me and said, "You've got a nerve." ' It is that sort of wicket, crucial, unorthodox and provocative all round that most pleases Botham. England won the match by seven wickets and swept the series. For Botham, it had been a bumper summer: two centuries and 37 wickets in six Tests.

Close catch. Bruce Edgar c Botham b Edmonds at Nottingham. Ian took nine wickets and snapped up two catches in the match.

Botham's Test record to date

Batting and Fielding

Tests	I	NO	HS	Runs	Avge.	100s	50s	Ct
11	13	1	108	500	41.66	3	1	12

Bowling

Balls	Runs	Wkts	Avge.	BB	5W/I	10W/M
2554	1059	64	16.54	8–34	8	1

III. Journey Down Under

One of the most famous photographs of Botham, taken by Adrian Murrell during the opening Test of the 1978–79 tour of Australia, depicts the young Englishman pounding down the wicket, a shout on his face and his right forefinger jabbed in the air. Rodney Hogg is at the crease, bemused and scowling, as he gazes back at his stumps which are picked bare of their bails. The tableau is misleading at first glance, for Botham is neither venting his anger nor gesturing crudely to Hogg. In fact, two stories surrounding that photograph go a long way in explaining the make-up of the remarkable Botham.

Australia, batting first in the Test, were all out for 116 runs, Botham taking three wickets, including Hogg's caught behind. In England's innings, Botham enjoying a savage partnership of 95 with Gower, was finally adjudged caught behind for 49, off Hogg. Botham was annoyed. He had looked set for a good score. After the day's play, with England in a commanding position of 257 for eight, he sought out Hogg at a barbecue steak dinner later that evening on the field. 'Hoggy,' Botham said, 'you were bloody lucky, taking my wicket.'

Hogg is a naïve man, with a blank, perplexed look on his face, but he's as combustible as an arms dump and at Botham's remark he exploded. Botham's ball that had taken *his* wicket wasn't all that special, either, he said, and as a matter of fact he was prepared to lay down a wager. Whoever claimed the other man's wicket more often in the series would win a bottle of booze of his choice from the loser. The two shook hands, sealing their bet with cans of Foster's. Thus began a personal battle which, while not as acid as the one the previous winter with New Zealand's Richard Hadlee, was every bit as rewarding to Botham.

England were all out the next day, 170 runs in the lead, and it wasn't until the final day that Botham had his first crack at Hogg since the wager. Botham had bowled astonishingly all match, his deliveries swinging so wild and uncontrollably that Bill O'Reilly, writing a newspaper commentary, said he had never seen a man move the ball so much in the Australian air. The air, indeed, was heavy and humid and when Hogg came in at 261 for six, his team 91 runs ahead of England, Botham was exhausted. So were the rest of the England bowlers, not least Bob Willis, whose feet were raw and bleeding. Hogg soldiered on. The scoreboard ticked over. England needed a breakthrough. Finally, Willis decided that Botham would profit by another insult. From mid-off, he shouted as Botham returned to his mark: 'Call that quick? You're bowling like an old tart. You couldn't knock the petals off a tulip.' It did the trick. The very next ball, and yes, *woosh*, Hogg was clean bowled. Botham charged down the wicket, his lifted forefinger in an 'out' signal. He was one up in his battle with Hogg. Botham remained incited, took a second wicket in the same over and, shortly thereafter, Willis got the awkward Kim Hughes to close Australia's innings at 339. England, needing only 170 for victory, achieved it with seven wickets standing.

In the Second Test at Perth, Botham took no wickets: his short figures, 0 for 100, were nicely symmetrical but served a sobering antidote to the news from London that he, Ian, had come runner-up to Daley Thompson as the Sportswriters' Sportsman of the Year. It was the first time in 13 Tests – he was to do it only once more in 25 – that Botham had come up with such a handful of dust. The bowling conditions were ideal, too, with the odd swirl of wind and cloud cover, but Ian's performance was blighted by one rush of blood and bad luck. The blood-rush came in the first innings when Australia were wobbling towards an eventual close of 190 runs. The vaunted Peter Toohey, playing his finest knock of the series, was putting up the single Aussie resistance and Botham decided to blast him out with bouncers. Toohey was equal to the attack, however, and mauled Ian for 14 runs in one over on his way to an unbeaten 81. The bad luck came in the second innings when Graeme Wood skied Botham to

One-up towards a bottle of booze. Botham bowls the disconsolate Hogg for 16, in the First Test at Brisbane, to go ahead in their friendly tour battle in 1978–79.

Boycott on two successive balls, only to be dropped in the sun, shortly after which Boycott caught a third one – on a no ball. With the bat, Botham scored 11 and a savage 30, and was content to let the others, notably Willis and Gower, do the work as England captured the Second Test by 166 runs.

Man of the Match at Perth was Hogg, with ten for 66 runs, which put him on target to eventually set the Australian record of 41 wickets in a Test series against England. Botham was having little trouble with Hogg. The man who was nettling Botham was Jim Higgs, a leg-break bowler, who returned to the Australia side for the Third Test at Melbourne. Higgs twice took Botham's wicket at Melbourne, for 22 and 10, while his compatriots Hogg and Hurst were dealing summarily with the other Englishmen, bowling them out for 143 and 179.

England were in deep water from the start. Australia piled up a respectable first-innings total of 258, with Wood handling the England pace attack to reach his 100. Botham took three wickets that opening day and fell one short of setting an England bowling record. Ian didn't know it – not many people did – but his third wicket, the bails of John Maclean, was his 63rd wicket of 1978. This total fell one short of the most wickets taken in a calendar year, a rarely cited record set by Syd Barnes in 1912. Australia began their second innings on January 1, with a lead of 115 runs: and Botham resumed his plunder of wickets. Botham's first victim was Wood. He had been having enough trouble with the Australian, one place or another, but at last Botham felt he had found the chink in the man's armour. 'I reckoned that if you bowled from over the wicket, he left the ball very well just outside off stump,' Botham recalled, 'but bowling from round the wicket, it was my theory that he couldn't judge where his off stump was.' What was more, since Wood could deal with all the pace that Botham could offer, Botham felt, why not try a slow ball round the wicket? 'I gave him a *really* slow ball. He probably saw it coming but he played the shot about a quarter of an hour too early. He tried to sweep it, missed it and was bowled leg stump.' Wood was flabbergasted. So was Hendrick, who greeted Botham's wicket with cynicism. 'I'm surprised that ball had the pace to knock the bails off,' he said.

Hendrick had something to say about Botham's next wicket, too. Hendrick had bowled a long spell and had begun to tie down Hughes who, playing well, was stalled and frustrated on 48. Hendrick went off to change a boot. 'Brears put me on at Mike's end and I wanted to get the first ball up there, somewhere near straight,' Botham continues. 'It was nothing more than a loosener, but it was of a good length, pitching just outside the off stump. Hughes, as he often does, got impetuous with the first ball from a new bowler and he sort of walked into it and tried to smash it. It went straight to cover where Gower took an easy catch. When Hendo came back on the field he looked me straight in the eye and said, "No wonder they call you Golden Bollocks." ' Botham was to take another wicket in the innings, bringing his match total to six, but England failed to mount a reply. Australia won their first and only Test of the series, by 103 runs.

On Rest Day at Melbourne, Botham played golf with Trevor Laughlin, another pace-bowler with a muscular golfing touch, and returned to the hotel content to have out-driven him. Botham fraternises freely with rival players on tour and has the commendable capacity to take defeat in good heart. 'It's a bit of a pose that Ian dislikes certain cricketers,' his Somerset mate, Roebuck, will say. 'He doesn't try particularly hard against one team rather than another, as some of us do. He doesn't try

Hogg, bowled again and bewildered. Ian again gets his favourite Aussie, this time in the Third Test at Melbourne in 1978–79. Botham took six wickets, but England lost the match.

Surprise. Ian, delighted, bowls Australia's Graeme Wood with an outlandish slow ball in the Melbourne Test, 1978–79.

particularly hard against certain bowlers or batsmen, *except* when their challenge in some way becomes public and his dominance must be demonstrated.' Botham's tolerance does not extend to vulgar, rowdy crowds and of these, especially on The Hill in Sydney, he said: 'Some Australians are just like their country, big and empty.'

Sydney was the scene of the Fourth Test. It was where England won the Ashes and where Randall played the innings of his life, saving England and then putting them in command with a marathon innings of 150 runs. Botham did his bit in the match, scoring a powerful but judicious 59 in the first innings, 6 in the second, taking two wickets during a long and punishing spell with Hendrick and Willis off the field, and five catches. With the clarity of hindsight, two events in the match stand out. One was his 6 runs in the second innnings when, with the England recovery hanging in the balance, he chose to play a sheet-anchor role to Randall. It was a role for which he was roundly criticised in the Press, one respected English writer calling his innings 'a classic example of the futility of extreme defence'. Botham doesn't see it that way. When he came in, England were 237 for four, only 95 runs ahead. When he left, he had consumed an hour and a half and scored 6 runs: never before in his life had he stayed at the crease for that length of time without a six or even a boundary. Brearley later was to call Botham's innings a 'display of aggressive defence'.

Botham explains the innings that baffled his friends and critics. 'If people had been looking at the clock rather than the scoreboard they might have realised what I was trying to do,' he explained. 'Randall was going well, but he was getting tired and he wanted moral support. I went out and said to him, "Come on, Arkle, fight. Time is more important than runs." My sole interest was to stay in and eat up as much time as I could. It was a challenge. Nothing was going to get past me. They were going to have to dig me out. My brain got so committed to this mould of pushing forward that when it got fatigued after ninety minutes, I made a mistake. I misjudged a spinner from Higgs and popped it up to silly point. Perhaps I should have opened up at that point, but who won the match?'

The other event came on the last day, with Australia chasing an attainable 205 runs. Rick Darling, a ferocious puller of the ball, smashed a long hop from Emburey. Botham, who was fielding at short leg in a helmet, later took up the story: 'I was only a couple of yards off the bat and, before you say I was too close, look at some past films and you'll see I've often fielded that close without a helmet. Anyway, when I saw he was shaping up for the pull I tried to back off, then *whack* it was all over. Winchester Cathedral bells in the ear-holes: vibes and double-vision. Then everything went black.' Botham will turn snappy at arm-chair critics who scorn the helmet innovation. 'Don't ask me if I think I would have been killed. I don't *think* I would have been killed, I know I would have been killed if I hadn't had on the helmet.' As grim testimony to Botham's words the helmet, Brearley's, still carries a dent above the left temple.

When the Ashes were won – by the eventual 93-run triumph at Sydney – one climax was reached on the tour. The other came twenty days later at the beautiful Oval ground at Adelaide where England won the Fifth Test by 205 runs to assure themselves of winning the six-match series. Botham's anecdotes surrounding this match have been written in Brearley's *The Ashes Retained*: Botham's mulish refusal to follow Brearley's advice and wear spikes while batting but, during lunch, making no comment but putting them on. 'Though Botham sometimes initially seems reluctant to listen,' wrote Brearley, 'he does take a point.' And Botham's changing-room 'tiff' with Hendrick.

Botham had dropped Bruce Yardley off Hendrick and, after play, had been given a roasting by Hendo for not fielding with orthodoxy at second slip. Still, observed Brearley, 'they soon were drinking beer, replacing the fluid they had lost under the Adelaide sun'.

Botham's most lasting achievement at Adelaide was his mature, measured batting, a discipline he might have been rehearsing during those long tortuous innings at Melbourne and Sydney. He turned round the match with his 74 runs in England's first innings, an achievement that earned him the Man of the Match award. Botham took five wickets and, although none was Hogg's, it was in this match that he finally defeated his Australian friend by refusing to rise to his provocative early bouncers. Botham prudently waited until his tormentor had spent his forces, literally given up the battle, and only then did he begin hammering the Australian round the ground.

The series truly drifted to an anticlimax, Botham picking up four more wickets in England's nine-wicket victory in the Sixth Test at Sydney and when last seen, after stumps were drawn for the last time on the tour, Botham was touring the King's Cross area of Sydney with Hogg, having won his bet with the Australian: Botham had taken Hogg's Test wicket three times while Hogg only twice dismissed Botham. What kind of bottle did Ian choose as his prize? 'You know, that beggar never paid me,' Botham said months later. 'I'll have to see to that the next time I'm in Australia.'

Botham's Test record to date

Batting and Fielding

Tests	I	NO	HS	Runs	Avge.	100s	50s	Ct
17	23	1	108	791	35.95	3	3	23

Bowling

Balls	Runs	Wkts	Avge.	BB	5W/I	10W/M
2822	1626	87	18.65	8–34	8	1

SIX

A Thousand for England

The willow groves that stretch across the lowland of Essex, near Chelmsford, are the breeding grounds of cricket bats. A merchant buys the standing trees from local farmers, fells and splits the wood. He retains only the trunks below the boughs and sends them round the country to batmakers who dry them, cut them into basic 'clefts' and, in some cases, fashion them specially for top players.

Botham has such a bat. His is different from other bats, say, for example, Sunil Gavaskar's. It is interesting to compare the bats of these two great players and fairly easy to do so, for they were both made by Duncan Fearnley, the batmaker, in Worcestershire. They each have standard 'short' handles of $11\frac{1}{2}$ inches but there the similarity ends, surprisingly and dramatically. Gavaskar is a tiny man but, in his 100th wicket duel with Botham at Lord's, he had wielded a big player's bat: the blade is 23 inches from shoulder to toe and weighs 2 pounds 10 ounces. Conversely, the bat Botham is to use in the Headingley Test is feathery in his massive arms: the blade is 22 inches long, the bat in all weighs 2 pounds 8 ounces. Fearnley has a simple reason for Botham's choice of the lightish bat. 'Ian likes to give it a swish,' says the batmaker, 'he likes to whistle it round his neck.'

Botham's bat for the Third India Test at Headingley may be light, but, by his own standards, it is *heavy*. His most successful bat, for example, was the one with which he scored his first three Test centuries, the 103 against New Zealand at Christchurch in 1978 and the 100 at Edgbaston and the 108 at Lord's, both against Pakistan that following summer. It weighed 2 pounds 6 ounces. At the outset of the 1979 domestic season, Botham decided ruefully that there weren't many more centuries left in the old warclub. It had been split and glued too often. What is more, it was too light, about 2 pounds 4 ounces, simply because much wood had been sanded away from the blade during three factory visits for resurfacing. It was now much too light, even for such a swisher as Botham. In July, Botham retired the bat, gave it back to Fearnley and now the old cudgel resides in the batmaker's office, not far from a huge six-gripped, 3-pound club with which Clive Lloyd scored his record 242 not out against India at Bombay in 1975.

Not for nothing is Botham's new bat heavy (at least for him): to handle the spin of the visiting Indians, Venkat and especially Bedi, he felt he needed more wood and thicker edges on his bat and, accordingly, Fearnley fashioned him one. Botham found the bat had remarkable heft. 'It is heavier than I've ever used in my life,' he said, after

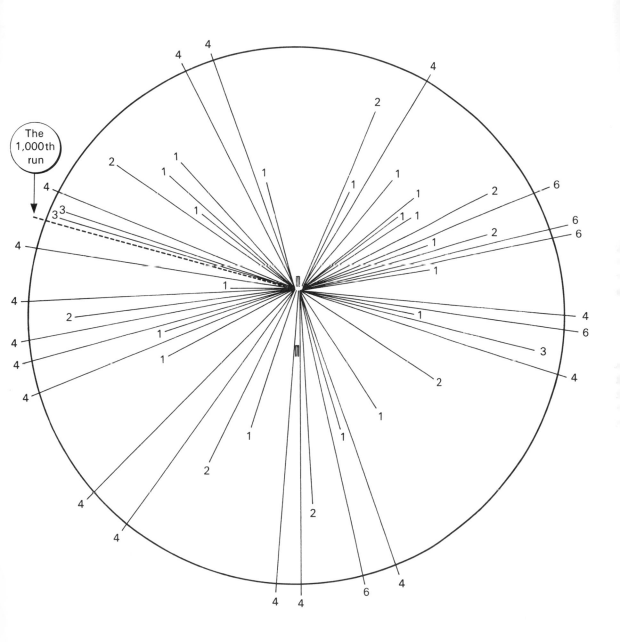

Shot chart of Botham's 137 at Leeds, together with the dotted line designating his 1,000th run, square cut in the next test at the Oval. For simplicity, Frindall's chart is keyed off a single end of the wicket. Note 360° distance of shots.

75

trying it out in the nets that day a fortnight later at Lord's. 'Yet, because of the balance, it feels lighter in pick-up.' Finally, the texture of the wood is different, one bat from the other. Gavaskar's is a young, sprightly piece of wood; it has eight grains across the face of the blade and is made up of some 14 per cent moisture, characteristics which combine to make it springy and softish, likely to last through many seasons. Despite its weight, it is rather subtle, a rapier. By comparison, Botham's bat is an old, ready-made broadsword: fifteen grains trail down the blade and only 10 per cent of its weight is moisture. It is a blunt and unyielding bat, and may not last long.

Botham's new weapon, his Excalibur, capable of consuming anything before it, is with him on the morning of August 16 as the England side sit in the changing-room at Headingley. In the Press that morning there was conjecture about Botham's Test double: he has two turns at the crease in the match, will he reach the 140 runs he needs for the record? It has been noted that no fewer than 17 Test players have done the double, dating back to 1896 when the Australian George Giffen reached the mark in a match against England at Old Trafford. In his splendid *magnum opus, The Wisden Book of Test Cricket 1876–77 to 1977–78*, Bill Frindall cites them all:

Country	Tests	Runs	Wkts	Tests in which Double was achieved
ENGLAND				
T. E. Bailey	61	2,290	132	47
A. W. Greig	58	3,599	141	37
R. Illingworth	61	1,836	122	47
W. Rhodes	58	2,325	127	44
M. W. Tate	39	1,198	155	33
F. J. Titmus	53	1,449	153	40
AUSTRALIA				
R. Benaud	63	2,201	248	32
A. K. Davidson	44	1,328	186	34
G. Giffen	31	1,238	103	30
I. W. Johnson	45	1,000	109	45
R. R. Lindwall	61	1,502	228	38
K. R. Miller	55	2,958	170	33
M. A. Noble	42	1,997	121	27
SOUTH AFRICA				
T. L. Goddard	41	2,516	123	36
WEST INDIES				
G. St A. Sobers	93	8,032	235	48

Country	Tests	Runs	Wkts	Tests in which Double was achieved
INDIA				
V. M. H. Mankad	44	2,109	162	23
PAKISTAN				
Intikhab Alam	47	1,493	125	41

Two records in this group stand out as relevant. They are clearly within Botham's sight at Headingley or, failing that, in the final India Test a fortnight later at the Oval. The first was the fewest Tests an England player had taken to reach the double: 33 Tests, reached by Tate in 1931. Of Tate, Botham knew nothing, save the name, for the man had died when Ian was an infant – and much the pity, for they were cut from the same heroic bolt of cloth, big, strong and courageous. Tate, who is considered by many to have been the finest fast-medium bowler between the wars, was a tidy craftsman who was said to have never bowled a bad ball throughout his career with Sussex and England. He didn't bowl a Test ball at all until he was 28, partly due to the interruption of the First War and partly to miscasting himself for years as a spinner. Once chosen, Tate launched into an astonishing start: 65 wickets in his first ten Tests. His Australian tour of 1924–25 was particularly rewarding: 38 wickets. He was particularly valiant on that tour, too, for at the Adelaide Oval he tore the nail off the big toe of his landing foot but soldiered on with blood seeping through his boot. It took Tate 20 Tests to take his 100th wicket, one more than Botham, but with surprisingly few batting opportunities, 33 to reach his 1,000th run. 'What Maurice had in common with Ian,' John Arlott will tell you, 'was a terrific physical build, this great big bottom and the will to fire the ball into the pitch. As batsmen, they were pretty much alike, too, although Maurice was clumsier. He was a prodigious straight driver of the ball and a fine cover driver. But he couldn't hook like Ian.'

The other record, a stiffer challenge, was the fewest Tests *anyone* had spent in reaching the double: this was held by the Indian Mulvantrai Himmatlal Mankad, known as 'Vinoo'. Mankad completed his double in 1952 in his 23rd Test, having reached his 1,000th run while scoring a stunning 184 in the second innings against England at Lord's earlier in the year. Mankad was a burly, bow-legged workhorse (he bowled 97 overs in that 1952 Test at Lord's) who would bowl with his spinning finger until it bled. A brilliant cricketing prospect, he is said to have played so impressively during the unofficial 1937–38 matches against Lord Tennyson's touring England side that Tennyson rated the 20-year-old already worthy of a place in a World XI. The career of Mankad, like Tate's, was interrupted by a World War: it wasn't until the age of 29 that he made his Test debut, against England. He died at the age of 61 in Bombay in 1978.

Botham knows of this record, but not of the man, as he awaits the return of his captain, who has tossed up with Venkat. England win. Boycott and Brearley get away to a gratifying start and reach 53. In the course of four overs, though, the bottom drops out: Boycott goes, followed by Gooch, then the captain and when Gower is given lbw for his first Test duck, the side looks to be in rout: 58 runs with four wickets down.

Maurice Tate, Sussex and England, held the double record for England players: 100 wickets and 1,000 runs in 33 Tests.

Vinoo Mankad, the supreme Indian all-rounder, set the target for Botham: in 1952, Mankad completed his double in his 23rd Test.

Brearley, on his return to the pavilion, has told Botham that if the light were to get bad while he is batting and he is offered the option of whether or not to come off, he was to take it. He is to do so to stop the rot and, more important, to buy time to allow the seaming wicket to dry out a bit. In passing this firm advice, Brearley is making a veiled reference to the previous summer at Headingley when, although the series was already won against the Pakistanis, Edmonds declined the offer of bad light because he felt in form at the crease. Tactically, Brearley feels this had been wrong for the team. It wasn't going to happen again. The captain's order is understood, albeit silently, by Botham.

Botham has learned little by watching the bowlers: the dressing-rooms at Headingley, like those at Old Trafford, do not present a useful view down the pitch and, what is more, the picture on the dressing-room television set is flip-floppy and cloudy. Botham has been gazing idly out of the window, all padded-up, thinking of nothing. 'I was trying to get keyed-up by the general atmosphere of the game,' he said later, 'I was getting into a mood.'

At the fall of Gower's wicket, Botham clumps down the wooden stairs to the field, and, although his team-mate casts an eye at the sky as they pass, Botham is confident. There can be few sportsmen who bring such unconscious optimism to their trade as Botham. 'Headingley is a pretty lucky Test ground for me,' he will say, although such a comment does not altogether hold up: in three Test innings there he may have taken nine wickets but in two batting appearances he has scored only four runs. It is part of his nature, though, to forget failure and remember success. Even his view of the ground reflects this rosy outlook. 'There may be a big boundary at Headingley,' he will say, 'but the outfield is quick.'

India's policy towards Botham as a batsman is uncomplicated and, given the man, perhaps predictable. Bedi had outlined it at the team meeting before the Edgbaston Test. In his opinion, to get Botham out did not require a particular field or a ball or a bowler. 'We don't have to "feed" him,' said Bedi, 'we just have to tie him down; the sooner the better, and maybe he'll do something stupid like trying to hit over the top. Remember, as soon as he comes in, he will try to get on top of a bowler.' Bedi's judgement was basically accurate except in this instance. With only ten minutes remaining before the end of the session, Botham has no intention of getting on top of anybody. He is there to survive and, meeting Randall in the middle, he says, 'We've got to fight this out until lunchtime.' Botham takes guard, middle and leg, before wandering up the wicket to tap down a few imaginary spike-marks. He decides to settle into an opening attitude of aggressive defence. Kapil Dev is himself in a mood of unbridled aggression. He has dismissed Gower and, in nine overs, has taken two other wickets at the cost of only 17 runs, bringing his wicket total to eleven for the series, only two short of Botham. His out-swinger is moving ominously in the patchy sunlight.

Botham is not a talker at the crease. He thinks that talking, as Randall talks, suggests vulnerability and any remarks he makes will probably be cheerful and therefore provocative. Mostly, he speaks to himself, and under his breath. 'Just block,' he says, gazing up at the swarthy Indian. 'Just block,' he repeats, sinking forward, practising the defensive shot at which he is becoming more and more skilled. 'What I am looking for, early on in an innings, is the danger ball, the ball that leaves you,' he will say. 'If you go over too far to cover it, you're in danger of the ball that nips back.' To such a ball, therefore, Botham tries to get his pad on the line, with the bat just behind the pad and covering for the ball that moves.

Dev's first ball is neither the danger ball that taunts Botham before leaving him nor, also fearful at this stage, the straight ball that compels the Englishman to play. It is a harmless ball that begins off stump and swings well away. Botham leaves it. Randall thereupon receives the first five balls from the medium-paced right-handed Amarnath, scoring a single off the last. Botham takes strike. He glances at the sky, which is increasingly overcast, and he thinks: the ball is going to do things, let's get to lunch. Amarnath comes in. It is to be the best ball bowled at Botham during his entire innings. Just short of a length, just outside the off stump. Botham, starting to go back to play the ball down, suddenly is beaten as the ball nips back sharply. 'It cut me in half,' he is to say later, 'four inches lower and it would have bowled anybody.' Amarnath's mouth drops open in disbelief at the behaviour of the ball. Botham smiles at Amarnath, as much to encourage himself as to annoy the Indian. Randall laughs as they join in the middle. 'Poof,' he says, 'I'm glad I didn't get that one.' Botham's third and last ball of the session, in the next over, is dabbed down towards the covers and he takes a quick single. He is pleased: the single not only has got him off the mark but out of harm's way, away from the strike. Botham is one and England 61 as they go to lunch.

The sky is overcast, the light poor when Botham returns to the middle at 2.10. He resumes his cautious ways but, after an interlude of 14 quiet balls, he breaks loose. A half-volley from Amarnath is treated with suitable disdain; the ball is smartly driven through mid-on to the boundary. It is Botham's first crisp shot of the innings and, in his

A page from the ball-by-ball account of Botham's innings at Leeds. Many of the notations, such as bowlers, batsmen, runs and time of day, explain themselves, but Bill Frindall has devised a detailed code to signify other aspects of the run of play: each dot is a ball bowled, the bold number is the runs scored from the shot, the number above it the area into which the shot went (see Clock).

ENGLAND v. INDIA at Headingley, Leeds   3rd TEST   16,20.8.79

Umpires: (H.D. BIRD) RUGBY STAND END · (B.J. MEYER) KIRKSTALL LANE END

1st DAY TIME	BOWLER (Rugby Stand)	O.	BOWLER (Kirkstall Lane)	O.	RANDALL — SCORING	BALLS	6s/4s	BOTHAM — SCORING	BALLS	6s/4s	NOTES	O.	RUNS	W.	'L' BAT	'R' BAT	EXTRAS
1·20	KAPIL DEV	10			RANDALL	3	—	BOTHAM	(no cap)	—	M8 NB5	24⁵	58	4	0	0	8
21			AMARNATH	7	P ⁹E · · · · 1 ·	8		·	1	1	M9	25					
26	"	11			LB X · · · ·	13		3s 1 · · ·	2		• Nearly bowled	26	59		1		
			AMARNATH	8		16		P · · · · · ▬	3	1	Ⓛ 2HR→	27	61	4	1	1	9
1·30 LUNCH	LUNCH										M9 NB5 LUNCH						
2·10	KAPIL DEV	12			IE 6F · 1	17		· · · ⊙ · ·	9		overcast; light poor M10	28					
2·14			"	9	⁷1 ·	22		⁷ · · ⁴ ·	12		Ⓝ NB6	29	62		2		
19	"	13			⁸1 · · · · 1	24		·	18	1		30	68		3	5	10
23			"	10					19			31	69		4		
27	"	14			L 3s 1 x · · · ·	29		³ˣ 2 · · · ·	23			32	72		5	7	
30			"	11				· 3	24			33	75		8		
35	"	15			x 3 3 · · · · · ▬	35			30		M11	34					
											M12	35					

Symbols: B Bye, E Edged stroke, EP Edged ball into pads, L Hit on pad, LB Leg Bye, M Maiden, NB No ball, P Hit on pad, no appeal, S Sharp (quick) single, X Played and missed, Y Yorker, Bouncer. W signifies the fall of a wicket. (The extract is published by courtesy of Bill Frindall.)

ENGLAND v. INDIA at Headingley, Leeds — 3rd TEST — 20.8.79

ENGLAND 1st INNINGS

4th DAY TIME	BOWLERS (H.D.BIRD) RUGBY STAND END — BOWLER	O.	(B.J.MEYER) KIRKSTALL LANE END — BOWLER	O.	BATSMEN SCOREBOARD LEFT — SCORING	BALLS	6s/4s	SCOREBOARD RIGHT — SCORING	BALLS	6s/4s	NOTES	O.	RUNS	W.	'L' BAT	'R' BAT	EXTRAS
12·27	AMARNATH	13						• · · 3	72		• RO chance (MILLER) ump. Bird fell over	51		5			17
31			GHAVRI	17	· · ·] 7	36		x 3 8 · 4]	75	1/5	M16	52	148		24	46	
36			"	14				7 5 · · ·	81		BEDI off for one over – sub Yajurvindra	53					
40			"	18	7 · 1	38		5 8 4 LB 46 · ·	85	2/6	M17 BOTHAM'S 50 in 121 mins (LB)	54	160		25	56	18
45	BEDI	1			· · · · · ·	43		2 3	86			55	163			59	
48	AMARNATH (Round wkt)	15						6 EP 4 · · · ·1	92	2/7	4 HR→	56	168			64	
52	"	2						3 5 · 4 · · · x	98	2/8		57	172			68	
54	"	16			9 1	44		x P 7 · · ·1	103			58	174		26	69	
57	"	3			8 EP · · · · · ·1	49		6 1	104	2/8		59	176		27	70	
1·02	"	17			E ___ W	53	3				Botham bat repairs • Hard chance (Sh. leg CHANDRA)	59⁴	176	6	27	70	18
03			EDMONDS HELMET-CAP												0		
05			"	17	· : ·	2					M18	60					
06			"	4	P P P	7		8 ·	105			61	177			71	

09			"	18	P 7 3	12		6● 1	106		● Dropped Mid-on (VENKAT - diving)	62	178			72	
13	"	5						8 P 9 1 6 · 2 · · 4	112	3/9		63	190			84	
16			"	19	2 E 2 3 2 · · 2 2 ·	18						64	196		6		
21	KAPIL DEV	23			L	23		2 1	113			65	197			85	
24			"	20	.	24		5 7 2 8 · · ⊙ 4 4 4 ①	120	3/12	NB NB 9	66	211			98	19
29	"	24				24	-	7 1 6 4 · · · ·	126	4/13	BOTHAM'S 100 in 170 mins - 99* before lunch in 123 runs of 95 balls	67	221	6	6	108	19
1·33	LUNCH											LUNCH					
2·10			VENKAT	1	4 1	25		3 4 2 6 ·4●2 2 ·	131	4/14	BOTHAM'S 4s in Tests ● (previously 108)	68	230		7	116	
13	KAPIL DEV	25			● 8 O2 · · 1 · ⊙ ·	31		8 1	132		● Dropped 1st slip (VISWANATH) NB to (NB) ct. VENKAT (gully)	69	233		8	117	20
18			"	2	6 · · ·	34		3 · · 1	135			70	234			118	
20	"	26			2 4 · · · ·	39	1	↑9 · ①	137		NB 11 5 HR	71	239		12	119	
24			"	3	· ·	41		6 5● 2 · 6 2 1	141	5/14	● Dropped CHAVHAN - running from long-on	72	248			128	
27	"	27			1● 1 4 · 1	44	2	2 3 1 4 ·	144	5/15	● Dropped 2nd slip (VENGSARKAR)	73	258		17	133	
32			"	4	LB · ·	46		3 · · · 4	148	5/15	(LB) VENGSARKAR off-field -	74	263			137	21
34	BEDI	6			7 RO · · 1	49	2	3 · ·	150		sub YAJURVINDRA. (Batsmen crossed)	74[5]	264		18	137	21
36					TAYLOR	HELMET-CAP									0		
38	"	6				1						75					
39			"	5		1	-	4 · W	152	5/15	BOTHAM batted 201' M18 NB 11	75[2]	264		0	137	21

view, 'it is nice to feel the ball on the bat'. With that shot, his confidence is renewed, he feels himself in a bellicose mood. 'You're not good enough,' he remarks at Amarnath, under his breath, 'I'm going to take you apart.' Two balls later, he pushes a two through gully. During a maiden over from Kapil Dev he survives two lbw appeals and then he turns Amarnath for two to bring his total to 9 runs. That ends his day of scoring for, at 2.45, rain stops play which later is abandoned. Botham is 9, Randall 11 and England 80 for four.

There is no play on the second or third day, due to the rain, and each day Botham plays golf. This violates a credo observed by some purist batsmen: never play golf during the cricket season and *never ever* play in the middle of a batting innings. 'There is a lot of crap talked about golf upsetting your batting technique,' Botham will say. 'You've got to switch off, you've got to do something and for me golf is relaxing.' It also is engaging; Botham has had a fierce running golfing competition with Ken Barrington, a team official, through Pakistan, New Zealand, Australia and many points in England. Botham, playing off a handicap of 11, loses badly to Barrington that weekend and, perhaps because it is not his front-line game, he makes excuses, something he would never do in cricket. 'I probably played the worst that I've ever done in my life,' he says later, 'but I was knackered. I was tense. It had been a long season and there was an important Gillette Cup match coming up in a couple of days between Somerset and Middlesex.'

On the fourth morning, some ninety-four hours after coming off, Botham and Randall are back at work and with only two days left the match was all but dead. Once again, the weather is cold, the sky overcast and, once again, Dev is swinging the ball, Ghavri seaming it off the wicket. The Indians have the batsmen on the defensive and at the end of three overs they claim their first wicket of the day: Ghavri bowls Randall, tangles him up behind the legs for 11. Botham has inched up to 13, England are 89 for five.

Bedi, in the infield, studies Botham. The Englishman stands, leaning on his bat, ankles crossed, viewing nothing. He is preoccupied and this is written on his face. It is a look of aggression. We are in for an interesting spell, Bedi concludes, Ian has decided that the best defence is to attack. The Indian has correctly interpreted his rival's demeanour, for Botham is considering the state of the game: while building an innings with Randall, he had been right to leave many balls he normally would have played, Botham thinks, but once Miller is gone there won't be much batting left in the side. I'm going to play.

Miller comes in. In the past, he has joined Botham in some long, middle-order stands, the most successful of which was enjoyed the previous winter in Adelaide when they put on 122 runs against Australia in the Fifth Test. Miller remembers the jokey ease with which they batted together. Botham had called him to the middle at a crucial moment that day and said: 'Christ it's hot, Dusty, let's make out we're having a chat for a while and hold up the play.' Botham is gifted in taking off the heat, real or figurative, with the irrelevant remark. Furthermore, if Botham is in 'good nick', Miller especially enjoys batting with him. Under a Botham bombardment, the opposition tend to take off the pressure by leaving fielders out to Miller as well.

The runs are there for the taking. At this stage, though, Miller emphasises the need for England to consolidate their innings. 'We've still got a long way to go,' he says in the middle, 'let's not try too many shots.' Botham nods, barely listening: he is not of the same persuasion. If the ball is there, he says to himself again, I'm going to hit it. Besides, he is beginning to feel a little claustrophobic: I want to smash some balls and get the fieldsmen pushed back.

It is odd that after about four days' rest Dev and Ghavri suddenly appear tired. They soon are bowling short balls, half-volleys and full tosses and when Ghavri bowls a rare, goodish delivery, Botham edges it, just a nick, into his pad. The Indian is up with a shout: lbw! Botham holds firm. Batsmen will often wave their bat at this point to indicate a touch but Botham, perhaps surprising for such an uncompromising competitor, rarely tries to influence umpires. Umpire Barry Meyer gives him not out. Botham takes a single off the next ball and remarks to Meyer: 'That was close, wasn't it?' Meyer nods and precisely describes the shot: 'An inside edge, nicked onto the pad.' Botham's confidence in both himself and the umpire is reinforced. It is a good feeling and in a spirited mood of attack he faces what is to be an eventful over from Ghavri: he plays and misses and then, when the Indian digs in a short ball that doesn't get up, he neatly whips it away behind square leg for two. He turns a boundary down the leg side and, taking the measure of a half volley on leg stump, drives a three through mid-wicket. Miller immediately takes up the attack on the crumbling bowlers, scoring ten off the following over, all from full tosses from Dev. The two batsman meet. 'Look,' says Botham, 'I've been out here batting an hour and a half. How is it that you are getting the full tosses?' Miller laughs. 'I'm lucky,' he says, 'fancy a flutter tonight?' They discuss the merits of the casino at the Dragonara Hotel, where the team is staying in Leeds. Perhaps a small innocent visit to the table would be in order. The partnership is in good heart: Botham 28, Miller 22 and England 127 for five.

In two overs, the pair have scored 19 runs but suddenly, during the next half-hour, the balance of power swings to Botham. In that time England face 50 balls, Miller receiving only nine of them, of which he dabs away three to relinquish the strike. 'I was happy enough with this,' Miller recalls later, 'because by now the bowlers were *really* looking tired. With all his power, Ian could take advantage of it more than I could.'

Botham does indeed take advantage of the wearying Indians. In his eagerness he plays and misses three balls from Ghavri, all outside the off stump and then is given the strike by Miller. Third ball, facing the wilting Dev, Botham hits a straight drive for four. 'When I'm in that frame of mind, I don't care who is bowling,' he says later. 'I'm relaxed and I can see the ball well. I can see it early.' The next ball from Dev, a long hop that doesn't get up, is seen especially early. Botham gets quickly into position, waits, hooks it awesomely, shoulders back and left foot high off the deck. Savagely struck, the ball rises over the fieldsmen, over the boundary, over the edge of the pavilion and drops with a clatter into the players' car park, not far from Botham's own car. The six, one of the biggest ever seen at Headingley, lifts Botham to 40, his partnership with Miller to 50 in thirty-eight minutes and England to 141.

Bedi's worst fears have been confirmed. Botham is on top of the bowlers and enjoying it. What is more, he is in good rhythm. In the field, Bedi recognises that India are in trouble. With Dev and Ghavri being manhandled, he thinks, what are the prospects for the spinners, for myself and Venkat? Dev attempts to fight off the mauling: he bowls a bouncer which lifts so high that even Botham, anxious to attack, leaves it alone. The following ball, the last of the over, Dev appeals for an lbw. 'I heard the shout, but it didn't concern me,' Botham later recalls; 'all I was looking for was the next ball.' This is enough for Dev; he comes off.

Two overs later, Botham nearly runs out Miller. The field at that stage is defensive: two slips and the rest of the fieldsmen pushed out. Botham hits a ball into the off-side field and, reckoning the ball will roll wide of Sharma, shouts 'Yes'. He realises right away that he was wrong, there is no run in it. 'No,' he bellows but Miller is away, head down. 'No,' he shouts again, and Miller turns and scrambles back, safe only because the ball has skipped past the stumps. Botham puts his hand up in apology: my fault, bad call. Miller accepts it and soon dabs down a single to give up the strike; Botham takes five runs off the rest of the over and, five minutes later, Botham is dishing out to Ghavri the same merciless treatment he recently had given to Dev. It goes this way: first ball of an over, Miller pushes out a single and the batsmen change ends. Next ball, Botham straight-drives the chunky left-armer, a sharp, perfect blow, rather like a fighter's left cross, that just misses the non-striker's stumps. This is followed, in the metaphor of boxing, by the knock-out punch: Ghavri's third delivery is short, bouncer-length, but rising only as high as Botham's chest, and outside leg stump. It has little pace and Botham hammers it with a big, measured hook. It is a searing shot, just behind square, flatter than the last six, but easily carrying the boundary. Ghavri ends the over with an appeal, feebly shouted, for an lbw. Venkat responds as he did before: Ghavri comes off. Botham now is 56, England 160.

The wily Bedi is soon on, with Amarnath. On a turning wicket, Bedi fancies his chances against Botham. The veteran Indian is much like the Englishman in that he revels in a personal duel, mongoose versus snake; in a one-against-one conflict with Botham, he feels he knows his prey better than his prey knows him. 'In my opinion,' Bedi will say, 'quite a lot of Ian's batting is preconceived. For instance, if he thinks I am going to toss it up, he will go for it, whether I toss it up or not. Sometimes he will get away with this and sometimes he won't. But by the end of the day the percentages will be against him. It depends largely upon how long his luck holds.'

Equally, Botham relishes the challenge of Bedi, is excited by the Indian's cunning variations, his brave willingness to toss up a ball; in all, he deeply admires the intriguing intelligence Bedi brings to his bowling. Geeing himself up, eager to get on with the battle, Botham taunts the Indian. 'Come on, Rag-head,' he says silently, 'you're not good enough to get me out.' (In passing, it should be noted that Botham was uneasy that this anecdote should be used in the book. He maintains high respect and affection for the Sikh and wonders if such an irreverent reference to the *patka* might bring offence. 'I don't want to offend,' he will say, 'I'm just psyching myself up.')

Against Bedi, it is Botham's plan to 'mess up his length' and 'knock him off his line' by attacking his spin – and by doing so straightaway. 'If you allow Bedi to settle in and get into his rhythm, he's a lot harder to get hold of,' Botham will say. 'Also, if you attack his spin, the field will spread and there will be lots of ones around.' Botham believes he will achieve these unsettling aims by coming down the wicket, by using his feet adroitly and even by hitting Bedi over the top. But to attack Bedi wantonly is hazardous. The foremost of hazards in this respect is to be sucked into attempting to drive Bedi's big, awkwardly flighted ball, the one that bounces too short to be comfortably driven.

Botham retains strike as Ghavri bowls a leg-bye on his last ball of an over. He then attacks Bedi first ball. It is a short ball, not quite a half-volley, and in-swinging: just the ball calculated to lure Botham into driving. Instead, Botham rocks onto his back foot and plays it with smug correctness, chopping it through the open gully for three. Miller,

Into the car park. Ian blasts his first six off Kapil Dev, during his awesome innings of 137 at Headingley. The shot, which Ian read early, raises him to 40 runs.

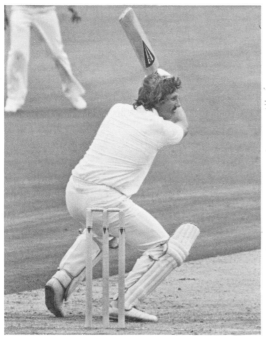

He stoops to conquer. Botham square drives to the boundary off Ghavri.

Gone again. Ian hooks his second six, this one off Ghavri, in his century run. The ball, pitched at bouncer length, didn't get up and attacked with sweet measure. This blow brought him to 56 runs.

tied down by the left-arm Indian's slow, probing, fly-fisherman's accuracy, is unable to nudge the strike back to his partner. Botham still enjoys his last shot off Bedi.

Botham grins, aware of the hoots of admiration that surely greeted this shot back in the England changing-room. His team-mates admire his skill and, more, his willingness to learn from his mistakes. The mistake they are alluding to this time was committed the summer before: in the Test series against New Zealand he had got out, more than once, trying to sweep the left-arm spinner Boock. Seven balls later, Botham's attention returns to the inscrutable Bedi. The Indian ambles to his mark, his shoulders loosely swinging as he strides in his own special way, shirt open and chin high, as though nothing in the world had happened to his earlier ball. Botham smiles; he thinks: Bish, you sly old sod, you're throwing it up a bit too early, aren't you? You thought you would catch me down the wicket and you didn't and it cost you three runs. Botham gets set for the next ball.

In the Press Box, Ted Dexter closely watches the action. 'The great thing about Botham is that whenever he picks up his bat he picks it up straight, vertically, with the tip of his bat directly above his hands,' says Dexter. 'His hands are cocked, loaded and ready to go. He's ready to hit every ball: if it's a bad ball he can attack, if it's a good ball he can defend. I've looked long enough at lots of good players to realise that anyone who picks up his bat this way gets good timing. It's the difference between an ordinary and a great batsman.' Bedi's ball comes. Botham is well balanced. He drives the ball, *slap*, along the ground to the boundary. Botham is satisfied: off Bedi's first two balls he has scored comfortably. He has won the first round with the Indian. He is 63, England 167.

Suddenly, though, Botham isn't satisfied. Nagging swiftly in his memory, and through his forearms, is the impure *slap* feeling of the last drive. It had been well timed, but slightly mis-hit. Botham studies his bat then holds it aloft, signalling the pavilion with it and making a tape-wrapping motion round the blade with his other hand. In making his last shot, he had cracked the edge of the bat near the toe, just a hair-line fracture, but one that needs attention. In the pavilion, Hendrick recognises the appeal and rushes into the physiotherapist's room where Bernard Thomas finds a roll of white medical tape. Hendrick meets Botham on the field. The tape is wrapped three times round the bat blade. Botham is ready to carry on. But, for his partner, the end is in sight. Facing Bedi, Miller plays a ball to short leg where Chandra puts down a hard chance. Four balls later he tries to steer a wide, shortish ball from Amarnath to third man and is caught behind. Miller is gone for 27 while Botham now stands at 70. Their partnership has been worth 87 runs in 80 minutes. England are 176 for six.

'Bish is turning a few,' Miller remarks to Phil Edmonds as he passes the incoming batsman. It is 1.03, just thirty minutes before lunch, and Edmonds bears the message to sensibly play out the session. Bedi indeed is turning a few, drifting his spinners into Edmonds who, not 100 per cent certain of the line, thrusts his pad forward safely to four early balls. He settles in and, next over, Botham is back on the attack. Bedi is bowling at him, from round the wicket. The first ball pitches well up, just outside leg stump. Botham sees the line of the ball early, comes out, and is there waiting for it. At the other end, in amused amazement, Edmonds watches what he later describes as 'technically, a very interesting shot'. In truth, it is an astonishing shot that baffles his mates in the pavilion. Botham would be expected to put his foot up the line of leg or even middle stump in preparing to hit the ball but, reading it so quickly, he plants his foot outside the line of leg stump, 'opens up' and instead of sweeping the ball behind square, pulls it massively in front of square leg. It rifles off the bat.

Without looking up, Bedi says to himself, 'That's gone', and indeed it is, soaring high into the darkening sky and into the car park. Bedi stops down the wicket, raises both arms high above his colourful *patka* and applauds. Bedi is a great applauder of sixes – at least sixes hit off himself. As one notices his team-mates are less generous in their acclaim, Bedi's clapping seems to be a gesture of true sportsmanship. This isn't quite right. 'I enjoyed Ian's hit, certainly,' he explains later, 'because it combined all the necessary ingredients of a perfectly hit six: strength, timing and luck. But, you see, clapping is my way of baiting a man. I clap him, hoping he will try it again – and hole out.' The Sikh's eyes twinkle. 'I do not, however, like my fielders to clap when I am hit for a six. I will do the clapping.'

Bedi's face resumes its emotionless mien as he gazes down the wicket at the Englishman; not a thought appears to be crossing it. Botham isn't fooled. Over the years he has come to suspect the motives behind Bedi's applause for a shot struck powerfully off him. 'When you hit Bishen hard,' Botham will say, 'quite often the next ball will be tossed up even slower, even higher, trying to get you to hit out.' Botham grins back at the Indian and in his mind he says: I know what you're planning, Bish. But there is no way, no way, I'm going to play at the next ball. No, we're going to play this game according to my rules. Botham settles down and the next ball, indeed, is given plenty of air, floating in as fat as a house. Botham moves forward, a picture of dour correctness, and blocks the ball with his pad. It dribbles down the wicket, dead. He looks at Bedi and blankly Bedi looks back. Botham has made his statement. Bedi has received it. Botham goes on to score six more runs off the over and is 84, England 190.

Botham is not to be stopped. Shortly thereafter, he is mauling Amarnath with a virtuoso performance: three fours in a row, struck right round the ground and all off goodish balls: mid-off, mid-wicket and the third guided deftly along the ground through the second slip area. Amarnath, unsettled, delivers a no ball which Botham neatly glances for a single to lift him to 98. That ends the over. It is 1.29, a minute before lunch. Time for one more over. Botham comes forward to meet Edmonds for a tactical chat. Dev is to bowl and, against such an onslaught from Botham, his fieldsmen are well out. It is an easy field against which to score singles. 'If they're there, I'll take them in ones,' says Botham, meaning he'll reach his century with caution, that is, if only Edmonds will keep giving him the strike. Edmonds agrees and settles back to watch. Dev comes in with his first ball. It is a rank long hop. Botham sees it early. He comes across, pounces on it and smashes a huge pull over mid-wicket. It is gone. Botham pauses to acknowledge the applause. He is on 104, having scored his century in 170 minutes. England are 217. At the other end, Edmonds is bemused: he laughs, thinking: some single. Botham recognising Edmonds' look, shrugs and chuckles to himself: I can't always play to plan. The next ball Botham steers through the gully area for four. He now has scored 23 runs off his last six balls, a record outburst even for him. He stands on 108 runs, England 221.

At this point, Botham sees the situation lucidly. There are four balls left before lunch. He needs 140 runs in his innings, which means he needs 32 more to reach his record: 1,000 Test runs and to reach the double. These runs will come in time, Botham reckons, either here or at the Oval. What he *doesn't* realise is that he is on the brink of another notable, and much more attainable, score. He already has scored 99 runs since play started at 11.30 and one more run off the four remaining balls would give him 100 before lunch. It would be the first time an Englishman had scored 100 runs in a morning session since Leslie Ames did it against South Africa at the Oval in 1935.

In the pavilion, the England players have worked out Botham's potential morning century and, while they wish him well over the course of the next four balls, they are delighted with his innings as it is and have no intention of trying to signal any message to score one more run. 'The last thing we wanted to do was to encourage Botham to aim higher,' Brearley is to say later, 'he aims high enough.' Brearley, amused, then pointed out what every first-class cricketer already knows: if only Botham knew that Vivian Richards, his friend, Somerset team-mate and fierce personal batting rival, was at that very moment moving towards a century before lunch against Middlesex at Lord's, he would open his shoulders and attack all four balls from Dev. He would attempt to bury Richards as well as the Indians.

So, in blissful ignorance, Botham spikes his guns and plays the next four balls with such supreme caution that shudders of agony pass through the Press Box. The first ball he blocks, the second and third skip harmlessly wide of the off stump. The last ball, the potential century-maker, is meekly blocked back to Dev. 'If I had known about the record,' he says off-handedly afterwards, 'I could easily have taken the single.' Botham is off to lunch, where he learns of his shortfall in runs over television. He lunches lightly on 99 for the morning, 108 for the innings. England are 221.

Botham loses no time in keeping the scoreboard ticking over when, third ball after lunch, he punishes a loose delivery from Venkat, off-driving it to the boundary. He now has his highest Test score, 112, and with a pair of twos puts the icing on the over, raising his score to 116, England's to 230. Botham's fifth and final six comes some twelve minutes later, off Venkat. Botham describes it: 'He threw the ball up a little bit. I went down the wicket, and everything was right. I moved into it in a normal arc and the ball carried over wide mid-off, and very sweetly.' The handsome stroke put him into the record books as he becomes only the fourth man, after Sam Loxton, Ted Dexter and John Edrich, to hit 5 sixes in a Test innings in England.

Botham, his body having wrenched round with the power of the blow, pauses as he uncoils and briefly looks at his mates on the pavilion balcony. Brearley and Willis reply with a great and genuine display of applause. Then, poking fun at their colleague, they make exaggerated defensive shot gestures: block, block, block the ball!

The allusion this time is to a remark that Viv Richards is alleged to have passed to Botham a fortnight earlier, after Botham had got himself into a tangle while playing the Indian spinners in the Test at Lord's. In that innings, Botham, trying to hit Bedi, had enjoyed a ration of luck when the balls just carried over the covers or landed dangerously short of extra cover. Botham thereupon went into a defensive shell. Blocking, he had got out ingloriously to Venkat. Richards had seen it all on television and later scolded his Somerset friend: 'What you going on about, man? Just 'cause you land a ball in the wrong place, doesn't mean you gotta stop playing your shots. You chicken? Keep on hitting the ball, man!' The rebuke suggested timidity. Ian had told the story against himself and his England mates had tickled the sting by picking up Richards's words in a sing-song West Indian accent. 'Once Richards had taunted him,' Brearley said later, 'there was no way I was going to dissuade Botham from attacking the spinners, even if I wanted to, because if there is one thing Botham seeks, it is Viv's admiration and praise.' On the field, Botham has read the reference and attempts to reply to it with a rude, two-finger gesture. It doesn't come off because of the clumsy mitten-shape of his batting glove. He is 125, England 245.

Botham's fortunes are soon to run dry. The next ball is guilefully held back by Venkat, and Botham, admittedly looking for another six, comes forward and lashes mightily at the ball. He mis-hits it, high on the bat, and the ball lifts and sinks towards long-on. Chauhan sprints in and, falling, nearly takes the catch. Botham runs two off the ball and then adds a single to complete the over on 128. The end is on the cards, though, when Bedi comes on to bowl to Edmonds. Edmonds blocks the third ball to mid-on, giving Botham the next three balls to reach his target of 140 and with it his 1,000th Test run. Botham plays and misses the first of them and then, artfully moving onto his back foot, he cuts the next ball straight to extra-cover. Emotionally pumped-up, he has hit the ball harder than he realises and bursts down the wicket, shouting: 'Yes!' At the other end, Edmonds is dumbfounded. 'No!' he shouts back, but his partner keeps coming. There is no way Botham is not coming through, Edmonds realises and, having hesitated, he is lost: he chooses to sacrifice himself and sprints towards the batsman's end. Sharma whips up the ball, pauses like a donkey between two bales of hay, and finally throws to Bedi at the bowler's end. Bedi receives the ball, almost certainly in good time to sweep away the bails and put an end to Botham's innings. But he throws to his wicket-keeper and there, at the striker's end, Reddy dismisses Edmonds with strides to spare. It has been a stupid, tired mistake and Edmonds curses Botham in a replica of good humour. He glances at Bedi. 'Bish, you're a very good lad,' he mutters. 'You kept Both going.' Edmonds is out for 18, Botham alive and not at all well on 137 and England 264 for seven, clearly out of danger.

Botham is out next ball he receives. Venkat, bowling with a six-three field on the leg side, delivers a straight ball just outside the off stump. An easy single is there, if Botham plays the ball on its merit to mid-off, but by now his concentration is rattled. He tries to hit the ball inside out, loft it over extra cover, and through the gap in the off side. He mis-times it, though, and the ball rises in a soft, doomed arc to Ghavri who only moves a step to receive it. Botham's innings is over. He raises his bat and starts walking. He passes Venkat, who is clapping his fine innings. 'Good ball,' Botham says to the Indian captain, 'you got me going for the shot — and it wasn't really on.' Lumbering towards the pavilion, striding through a bowl of applause, he is pleased with his innings. Only as he climbs the wooden stairs to the changing-room does he castigate himself. 'You idiot,' he says, 'if you had taken it in ones, you could have cruised it.' Botham's long voyage to 137 runs, falling three runs short of port, was achieved in 201 minutes and among the 150 balls he received were 16 fours as well as the 5 sixes.

'Ted Dexter was the last Englishman to hit so well; indeed it is hard to think that Jessop or anyone else ever hit a ball any better than Botham did here,' said John Woodcock of *The Times*, writing in *The Cricketer*. 'It was a great joy of an innings and saved the match from being no more than a damp and dismal memory.' Botham's departure at 2.39 on the fourth day left England 264 for eight and 15 minutes later England were all out for 270. The match, which again was to be stopped by rain, finally drifted to a draw on the last day and it wasn't until a fortnight later, in the final Test at the Oval, that Botham was to reach his 1,000th Test run and therefore his double. The record-setting shot, a square cut to the boundary, comes in the first innings off Bedi.

Botham arrives at the crease with England 148 for four and rather formally pushes a pad forward to a good-length first ball. The battle, mongoose against snake, is joined and Bedi brings Gavaskar into silly point, barely a breath away from Botham. Crowded, Botham is uncomfortable. He looks at the Indian fielder and thinks: you better watch out because the next ball is going through there, just to the left of you. Bedi wheels in. Here is his account of the ball: 'My second ball to Ian was a ball that deserved more caution from a man who had just come in. It was a good ball, too, bowled at the stumps, well up, and as Ian shaped to play it, I thought: "If he misses the ball, he is bowled. If he nicks it he is caught." What he did amazed me. One normally doesn't go for the square cut so early in the innings.'

The square cut is exactly what Botham goes for and he brings it off exactly as he had predicted under his breath: to the fieldsman Gavaskar. He moves deftly onto his back foot and cuts. The ball shoots past Gavaskar, on his left side, and flees to the boundary. Botham is four for the day, 1,001 runs. The Oval explodes. Bedi bounces down the wicket and this time, in unalloyed admiration, claps Botham high above his *patka* before embracing him. 'I should not have been surprised when he went for that shot,' Bedi was to conclude. 'Ian is a restless cricketer and whatever he does, he does in a hurry.' Botham has his double, and indeed in a hurry: he has done it in 21 Tests, easily beating the previous England record of 33 set by Maurice Tate and the world record of 23 held by Vinoo Mankad of India. Botham's achievement was nicely confirmed at the Oval the next morning when he picked up his pile of fan mail. In it were two telegrams. One, from Oxshott in Surrey, read: 'Hearty congratulations. (signed) Joey Peckham, Maurice Tate's daughter.' The other, from Bombay, read: 'Heartiest congratulations on your breaking my late husband's Test record. Wishing you all the best. (signed) Mrs. Manorama Vinoo Mankad.'

The blow that brought the double. Ian's historic shot, a square cut to the boundary, lifting his Test runs to 1,001, is scored off Bedi at the Oval.

SEVEN

And a Double for Somerset

At Leeds, the third India Test drifted to a draw on the very day the news came from Northampton: Essex had clinched the Schweppes county championship with a victory over Northamptonshire. Essex already had won the Benson and Hedges Cup and now Somerset, alone among counties, had not won a major competition. Botham brooded over this fact as he pushed his way through well-wishers in the Headingley car park. He neatly laid his England blazer on the back seat and, dressed for driving in a sleeveless sports shirt and clean jeans, climbed behind the wheel and buckled on his seat belt. He lit a cigarette. Soon we were threading our way through the streets of Leeds towards the M1 and southwards to London.

The Benson and Hedges Cup was a sore point among Somerset cricketers that summer. They had won their first three matches convincingly and in the fourth round faced Worcestershire at Worcester. The weather that day was poor. Cold and wet weather already had dampened Somerset's chances in the championship and, more painfully, there were bitter memories of losing the John Player League the previous summer by the difference of a 0·775 run rate. If they could lose on a technicality, someone pointed out in the changing-room, why couldn't they win on a technicality? A ploy was concocted. If Somerset scored a run and declared after one over they would guarantee themselves a superior wicket-striking rate in Group A and a place in the quarter-finals. The matter was discussed. A vote was taken among the players and, apart from two abstentions, the ploy was unanimously favoured. Captain Rose telephoned Donald Carr, Secretary of the TCCB at Lord's. Was such a declaration within the rules? he wanted to know. Would Somerset be punished for instigating it? Carr said it was within the rules but, over the phone, there was a misunderstanding as to what the outcome might be if he carried it out. Rose declared. Somerset were punished. They were disqualified by the TCCB for 'bringing the game into disrepute'. Most of the players were furious. They briefly considered legal action and an injunction to stop the subsequent quarter-final but, wiser heads prevailing, decided against prolonging the affair.

Somerset were still much alive in two competitions. On that day, August 21, they lay first in the John Player League, two points clear of Kent who they still were to play in one of their two remaining matches. In the Gillette Cup, Somerset faced Middlesex in the semi-final round the following day at Lord's and that was why Botham was hurrying down the M1 towards London. The South Yorkshire landscape opened up,

The champions to be in 1979. Somerset's team: (left to right, front row): *Neil Russom, Graham Burgess, vice-captain Peter Denning, captain Brian Rose, Derek Taylor, Viv Richards, Dennis Breakwell.* (Back row): *Keith Jennings, Hallam Moseley, Peter Roebuck, Joel Garner, Colin Dredge, Ian Botham, Vic Marks and Phil Slocombe.*

broad and green, spoiled only by the occasional march of pylons and the dark, satanic suggestion of the mills that might lie to the left or right of the motorway. The car soon swept past Exit 32, which marks the M18 and the way east to Doncaster. Botham said casually, 'I turn off here to go home.'

The remark was startling. Ian Botham of Somerset, the Yeovil boy, making his home in the North? He, his wife and their children live in the village of Epworth, on the Isle of Axholme, in what is now South Humberside but commonly regarded as Lincolnshire. Botham is proud of the restorations he and Kathryn have made to the old farmhouse. 'We know that our kitchen at one stage was an abattoir and our dining-room a sweet-shop,' he said, 'we can trace the history of the house back about 150 years and then it goes blank.' The village is friendly, with the Mowbray Arms and the Queen's Head Hotel, with a close friend and a farmer, Bob Keall, living across the lane from Botham's back door. 'The main attraction in my living up here is that I can get away from Somerset and switch off from cricket and relax,' he went on. 'I love Somerset, I honestly do, but when I'm down there I'm always made to think about cricket. In Somerset, people take me for *who* I am whereas up here I'm taken for what I am.'

95

Botham, the farmer, with Tigger, takes a turn on a tractor in South Humberside.

That the Bothams should make their home so far from Somerset, and so near to Yorkshire, unsettles many Somerset supporters. He neither speaks in the apple-round vowels of Peter (Dasher) Denning, the butcher's boy from Chewton Mendip, nor wears the same bucolic innocence of Colin (Herbie) Dredge from Frome nor excites the affection of the long-serving Graham (Budgie) Burgess from Glastonbury. Brian Rose, who was born in Kent, loves Somerset like no other man living and would happily live out his days walking his golden labrador along the sands at Weston-super-Mare,

96

although now it is annexed by Avon. 'Some people down here don't think Both's true Somerset,' says Rose, 'and they can't come to terms with it. He is brash, confident, sometimes arrogant – and brilliant. Somerset people don't see themselves in that way.'

Botham is by nature a Northerner. In a few years there, he has become part of the Epworth community. In the last General Election, he cast a postal vote for his local MP, the Conservative Marcus Kimball. He plays golf at Selby Golf Club. He plays and trains with the struggling Scunthorpe United football team. He tramps over the fields round his home, shooting rabbit, hare and pheasant, often inviting his friends, Hendrick of Derbyshire and England, and Breakwell of Somerset, to join in a party. Breakwell tells a story of the competitive nature of his friend: he and Botham once were walking back from a rough shoot when suddenly they saw, on the crest of a hill some 150 yards away, a hare sitting up in the rubble of a cornfield. Botham said he was going to get the creature and Breakwell, reckoning his friend would try a wild and distant shot at the hare, said he was mad. At that, Botham set out, running waist-high through the corn stalks. Two fields later he cornered the hare, shot it and brought it back by the ears. Botham, driving down the motorway, acknowledged the anecdote. 'If you use that story in the book, though, make sure you also put in that I ate the hare,' he said. 'Some silly sons-of-bitches would be delighted to think that I kill just for the sake of killing. I don't. I eat what I kill. Put that in the book, *I eat what I kill.*'

The s.o.b.s who vex Botham are those who claim he doesn't play as well for Somerset as he does for England. Statistics to support this come to hand. In the three seasons he has played for England, 1977 through 1979, his chronological first-class county averages have been: batting 30·95, 19·64 and 34·78 and bowling 23·54, 18·12 and 32·53. In that time, his overall Test figures were: batting 38·33 and bowling 19·61.

The quality of pitches clearly is a factor in this marked difference in performance. Rose agrees. What he said of Botham's 1978 performances for Somerset could generally apply to the three-year span. 'Ian's batting for us frankly has been a disappointment this season,' he said. 'He's been trying to hit the ball as though he is playing on Test pitches. And in the championship we're rarely playing on such high-quality pitches. Ian hasn't played himself in for us at all.' Botham finds no real fault with Rose's assessment but, interestingly, he has a commendable reason for any comparative slump in his county bowling. 'Sometimes I let Somerset down as a bowler because when I go on a wicket that is helpful to me, which generally is the county wicket, I'm still bowling as though I'm on a Test wicket, a batsman's wicket, and I screw myself up by improvising and messing around. I fight the county wickets as a bowler, and I needn't do. I should just come up and bowl and let the ball do the work for me.'

Botham's chief crime at Somerset, as he sees it, is trying too hard and therefore the worst s.o.b.s of all are the yaboos, awash with cider, who taunt him for not giving his guts for the county. A case in point, perhaps the most unfair and hostile barracking he has suffered in his six years at Somerset, was fresh in his mind. It took place during the Gillette Cup second-round tie with Derbyshire at Taunton in mid-July, just two days after the first India Test. Botham had toiled for 29 overs in the second innings at Edgbaston and, on arriving at Taunton, he was not fit to play. His feet, raw and bleeding, were treated on the eve of the match and again before he went onto the field to open the bowling. He said nothing of it. By the end of his first spell he began to wilt: his bowling, already uncertain, went haywire. In the 54th over the veteran David Steele

The one that got away. Ian, with his England bowling mate, Mike Hendrick, shooting near Botham's home in South Humberside.

took him apart. He smashed an errant leg-side delivery for four. Botham's shoulders dropped. A fan shouted: 'Come on, Botham!' Next ball, Steele swept another boundary. The shouts turned to hoots and two balls later Ian again was hammered for four. 'Yer at Summer-set now, Botham,' cried another fan, and a third: 'Go back to England!'

Rose sensed the head of steam building up in his wounded mate. 'I knew what was happening to Both,' he said later, 'but there was no way I was going to move in. If I had spoken to him, even *looked* at him, he would have felt under attack on two fronts, the crowd and his captain. I could never do that to him.' The last ball of the over Botham, enraged, pounded in and let fly with a would-be yorker. Steele picked it up clean, whipped it through the leg side for a fourth boundary. Botham carried on down the wicket, soaked in sweat, glaring at his enemies near the sight screen, beat them to the punch. 'F—— off!' he roared and drove a 'V' sign into the air. No one in the crowd answered back. It was an astonishing thing for a local hero to shout at his home crowd. Equally, it had been astonishing behaviour from a home crowd towards their hero.

'I got annoyed that day, as annoyed as I've ever got on a cricket field,' Botham said in the car. 'I was bowling my guts out but the harder I tried the worse I bowled and the worse I bowled the more the crowd got on my back. I don't think I've ever come nearer to walking into a crowd. The only regret I have is that it sounded like I was shouting at

98

supporters who were just as sorry as I was about what was happening on the field.' Botham's bowling was not costly that day. Somerset, led by Rose's unbeaten 88, won the match comfortably by eight wickets and carried his team into the quarter-finals of the Gillette Cup.

Brearley has spoken of 'the one thing Botham seeks', which is 'Viv's admiration and praise'. This search is seen both as a bane and a blessing in Somerset. When these two great players come together their fans avert their heads while, at the same time, with one eye open, watch a pyrotechnic display of batting, a cricketing Guy Fawkes' Day. The players share the anxiety. 'I never like to see Viv and Ian in at the same time,' says Rose, 'if you get the two of them going, each trying to outgun the other, it can be catastrophic. They both can go out in a blaze of glory.'

Just such a display took place in the Gillette Cup quarter-final on August 8 at Taunton. The opponent was Kent, a side loathed for its smug, toffee-nosed and perennial successes, not to say its committee's indecent haste in re-engaging its Packer players in 1979. The durable young Roebuck normally comes in at number four to stand as a buffer between the battling giants, Richards and Botham, but on that day Denning moved to number five which provided two batsmen to keep apart Richards and Botham. Somerset batted first and soon a comforting gloom settled over the pessimistic home crowd: in the 15th over Somerset were 45 for four as Botham came on to join Richards. Throwing away any notions of caution, the two blazed away from the outset: 11 runs of the first over. It was risky business, cigar-smoking beside the petrol pumps, but in 7.5 overs they had added an exact half-century. I-told-you-so was yielding to isn't-it-wonderful among the fans when Richards, flailing, was caught behind for 44. Somerset were back on their heels: 95 for five. Ian, on 22 at that point, added seven runs off his next six balls before being caught trying to smash a ball high over backward square leg. Somerset, 102 for six, again were in deep trouble. Their cause was salvaged by the loyal, grafting, old trooper Graham Burgess whose unbeaten 50 lifted his side to 190 all out. Somerset completed their most remarkable one-day victory of the year when Botham (3 for 15) and chiefly the amazing Joel Garner (5 for 11) blew away Kent for 60 runs, their lowest one-day total in history.

After the match, the Somerset players met in the changing-room. Rose was angry. What the hell had Botham been thinking about? Five wickets down, 25th over, and here he was smashing the ball up in the air? Botham hardly listened. Cornered, he fought back. The reason he got out, he replied, was not because he hit the ball in the air but because he didn't hit it *far enough* in the air. His explanation went like this: 'I allowed myself to be inhibited and I flipped at the ball, whereas if I had really *whaled* it, I would have got away with it.' The Somerset players were amazed. How could you fault such reason? Roebuck remembers the meeting and looks on Botham's behaviour there as a splendid microcosm of the man's reasoning. 'What Ian was saying was that far from attacking too much, he should have been attacking rather more. And, as always, because he is such a brilliant rationaliser after the fact, he was putting his case clearly and precisely and with wholehearted conviction. Some of us, who are supposed to be more intellectual than Ian, thought we could tear his argument apart. We couldn't – and probably for the same reason he can't be torn apart in cricket. He attacks. He dominates.'

The reckless double-barrelled attack of Botham and Richards is a continuing point of discussion in Somerset. Do they compete? Do they kill off each other? The statistics of the Richards–Botham partnerships are intriguing, if not sufficient to settle any arguments as to whether they ought to divorce for the sake of the children. The Somerset Committeeman, Mike Hill, has looked at their career partnerships. In one-day cricket, Richards and Botham were to come together sixteen times by the end of 1979. Their average stand has been 32·13 while, in these sixteen matches, Richards scored an average of 95·82 and Botham, perhaps muted by his famed mate, averaged 22·43. In first-class games, they have come together only seven times. Their highest partnership was 174 runs, in an innings when Richards scored 204 and Botham 62 against Sussex in 1977; it was their only partnership of more than fifty. Botham, who has little time for statistics, dismisses any thought that in the middle the presence of Richards has a bad effect on him. 'It just looks that way,' he will say, perhaps rightly, 'because we're both attacking players.'

Besides, as Botham was discussing Richards, he was also speeding from Leeds to London and watching a motorcycle policeman in the rear-view window. The cop moved up on the blind side and held steady alongside the passenger's door. He was clocking us. Botham held fast and the two men hurtled along in a dead-heat, mile after mile, until Botham sickened of the game. 'Hell's fire,' he said and, nipping round the motorcycle, swung into the slow lane. The cop burst past and signalled Botham to pull over. He trundled to the car window. Botham, he said, had been speeding. Ian built his defence round a broken speedometer. The policeman listened, finally interrupted. 'Never mind, Mr Botham,' he said, 'that was a well-played innings. Give me your autograph and we'll forget about it.'

Botham signed and resumed the journey, and when the policeman turned off the motorway he put his foot down on the floor. He gestured towards the dashboard of the car which was fitted out with a cassette player, a pile of tapes (Rod Stewart and The Boomtown Rats) and a radio. 'See if you can find something on the radio,' he said, 'and not Radio 3. I'm not Brearley. I'm Botham.'

The following day Somerset beat Brearley's Middlesex side in the semi-final of the Gillette Cup at Lord's. Bowling, Botham had little luck – although in an early over Mike Smith failed to make contact with six consecutive balls from him – and finished with no wicket for 28 runs, an economical enough performance. The Somerset bowling attack was left largely to Garner (4 wickets), with able support from Burgess (3), to subdue Middlesex for 185 runs. In reply, Somerset started well and coasted, reaching 99 before the loss of their second wicket. With the opener Denning still in, they reached 183 and the brink of victory when Botham stepped in. 'Botham was simply Botham,' said the *Guardian* the next day. Selvey's first delivery to him was a no ball. Botham pounced on his second, a half-volley, and smashed it in a triumphant arch over square leg and into the stands. He then sprinted to the other end and in a crushing bear-hug, grabbed up Denning, whose 90 earned him the Man of the Match award. The 10,000 fans up from Somerset foamed over the pitch. For the second year running, Somerset were through to the final of the Gillette Cup.

The Lord's triumph was enough to stir memories – nay, nightmares – of Somerset's 'Lost Week-end' of the previous year. The 1978 team had reached the Gillette Cup final and, alone on top of the table, were set fair to win the John Player League. It didn't happen. At Lord's on the Saturday they faced Sussex, a side now without Tony Greig. They went out and scored a hefty 207 but then, appearing only one breakthrough from victory, they let Sussex slip through to capture the Cup. Fate struck again on the following day. Somerset needed a victory over Essex at Taunton but they lost the match, by two runs, and the John Player title to Hampshire.

Against this black backdrop, Somerset returned to Taunton where on the following Sunday, August 26, they needed only to turn over Kent to be virtually certain of winning the John Player League. Kent, on the other hand, were hard on Somerset's heels in the table and a victory in the West Country followed by ones over low-flying Glamorgan and then Middlesex at Canterbury would present them with their fourth John Player League championship. The trophy itself therefore seemed at stake when Rose put Kent in to bat. Botham, all fire, soon had Bob Woolmer trapped lbw when Kent had only 4 runs on the board. The fire then went out of the attack, even Garner, fiddling with his new cap like a proud schoolboy, unable to come alight. He got nothing. Botham failed to take another wicket. Chris Tavaré, still hopeful of a place in England's forthcoming tour of Australia, and Graham Johnson consolidated for a second-wicket stand of 91 runs and Kent closed usefully at 194 for six wickets. In reply, Rose was lost hooking in the first over with Somerset still not off the mark. Denning was run out to leave the home side gasping on 20 for two and, with Richards pecking away, Botham came in to the nervous cheers of an overflowing crowd. He flaired – and failed – pulverising his first ball off Woolmer for six, cover-driving to the boundary and then, to the astonishment of his friends and team-mates, dragging a wide ball from Hills onto his stumps. After that, only the dour Burgess (20) and the inelegantly effective Garner (32) put up much resistance and Somerset did well to last out the forty overs, losing the battle by 64 runs. Two points in arrears, with two games to play, Somerset kept the war alive the following Sunday, with Botham away on Test duty against India at the Oval, when they defeated Derbyshire at Taunton. Somerset again faced a crucial Gillette/John Player week-end. Another lost one, or would they find their first trophy?

At the Oval, the fourth India Test and the series hung in the balance on Sunday. England, 103 runs clear after their first innings, were now 280 runs ahead with seven second-innings wickets still standing. Botham had reached his 1,000 runs with that audacious square cut off Bedi and, brutally, had gone on to hit a six and four boundaries to reach 38 before, heel up and driving, he was stumped by Reddy off his nemesis Venkat. Ian had been devastating with the ball, too: India had been bowled out for 202, Botham taking the feared wickets of Gavaskar, Viswanath, Ghavri and, finally, Reddy. He took two catches as well, the second one a display of pure acrobatic reflex, amazing for a man of his size, and the luckiest and most bewildering catch of his Test career. He had just caught Chauhan in second slip off Willis and almost straightaway Vengsarkar edged a ball, again off Willis. It rifled back, knee-high, ticked off Bairstow's glove, shot down, ricocheted off Brearley's toe cap and ballooned softly and agonisingly over Botham's head. Ian twisted backwards and, in a pretzel knot, caught the ball with his left hand as Bairstow circled round him. 'Don't ask me what happened,' Botham said afterwards, 'I just saw it and grabbed it.'

England resumed their second innings after Rest Day and Botham, arriving at the crease at 192 for four, looked forward to a long knock on the princely pitch. His hopes were snuffed. Before he had got off the mark he played a ball wide of Bedi on the leg side and looked up to see the non-striker, Boycott, thundering down towards him. Botham set out, head down to save himself, and failed to see his partner's signal to stop. Botham plunged on and was run out, comfortably, to record his second Test duck. His scoring was over for the Test summer. His 38 in the first innings had brought his Test total to 1,035 runs. The run-out did not appear damaging to the England cause at that point for, when Brearley declared at 334 for eight later in the day, India were left the chore of scoring 438 runs in 498 minutes to win the match and square the series. It looked an unattainable target but Gavaskar and Chauhan, with gathering resolution, set about chipping out 76 runs before close of play on the penultimate day.

The match was headed for a certain draw, the third of the series, unless the openers were soon rooted out on the final day. Botham had a feeling that the bowling task would be formidable. He had an overnight dream and, upon reaching the ground, he mentioned it to Hendrick. 'Gavaskar's going to get his double-century,' said Ian. 'Last night I dreamt I was bowling at him and when I looked up, there it was on the scoreboard: "No. 1 batsman, 200 runs."' Hendrick laughed. 'I hope you're wrong,' he said, 'because if you're not he's got a few runs to come yet.' They came in time and Botham's dream, like Gavaskar's premonition of becoming Botham's 100th Test victim, was to be fulfilled. The sturdy little Indian, dainty on his toes, started the day on 42 runs.

Chauhan clearly was the man to be attacked. Brearley soon began to strangle him, bringing seven close catchers round the bat. When the second new ball became available, Botham turned loose with bouncers. Gavaskar interceded, when he could, taking away the strike with quick, darting little shots. It was brilliant. India moved on. Hendrick came off with a damaged shoulder, a worse injury than suspected at the time. His departure reduced England's strike, diminished Botham's threat from the other end. Gavaskar's score climbed past Viswanath's 113, the highest India total in the series. Gavaskar and Chauhan, back on track, lifted their partnership to 213 and suddenly it ended. Chauhan went for 80, edging a slip catch to Botham, belly-high but neatly taken. The 213 was the highest first-wicket partnership in the history of the England-India Test matches.

Gavaskar soldiered on. He was tiring but, early in the afternoon, he not only had passed Botham's 137 but Boycott's 155, the highest score hitherto attained in the series that summer. By late afternoon it became a race between runs and available overs in which to get them. Vengsarkar was stepping up the pace: he and Gavaskar added a run a minute, 153 in all. With the statutory 'hour' of play remaining, India needed 110 runs to win and Vengsarkar, hitting out, was dropped by Botham in the deep. Ian swiftly made amends, catching the Indian at mid-wicket. India now were 367 for three wickets and Kapil Dev, who had scored the fastest century of the season in the tourists' opening county match in June, was sent in to flail away with Gavaskar. He flared out, for a duck. Gavaskar reached his double-century and, although fatigued, kept the scoreboard ticking over. India now wanted 55 off the last nine overs; just about maintaining the rate; they soon needed 49 off eight. Botham came back. 'Sunny was looking to score runs quickly, he was keen,' he recalled, 'so I tried to bowl a ball right up in the block hole. It pitched a bit short but he didn't time it well and just chipped it to mid-on.' Gower took the catch. India: 389 for four wickets. Gavaskar out for 221. The end came quickly. Botham pounded down on Yajurvindra Singh, had him lbw. Botham stopped a ball from Venkat's bat at mid-wicket. Next ball he ran him out. Botham sent Sharma back to the pavilion, another lbw victim. In the final over the keeper Reddy was in, India needing 15 to win. He hit a boundary off the first ball, got two more runs and then, nine runs from victory or a wicket from defeat, sprinted towards the pavilion and a draw. In a match which had started slowly and dragged its weary way towards conclusion the two central figures of the summer, Botham and especially Gavaskar this day, had finally infused it with drama. The awards, made by John Edrich, were of proper value. Sunil Gavaskar was named Man of the Match. Ian Botham, with seven wickets and four catches in the game, was Man of the Series.

Botham's Test record to date

Batting and Fielding

Tests	I	NO	HS	Runs	Avge.	100s	50s	Ct
21	28	1	137	1035	38.33	4	3	33

Bowling

Balls	Runs	Wkts	Avge.	BB	5W/I	10W/M
4896	2098	107	19.60	8 34	10	1

In the changing-room, Botham slumped on a bench and said little for a half-hour. Brearley sat with him, joking with him, lifting his young star from the empty depths of anticlimax. The England captain, speaking as Middlesex captain, gave Botham an assurance that his team would sweep aside Kent on the following Sunday and make way for Somerset to win the John Player League. Brearley later gave his balanced view on Ian Botham, the Test player, for he had been captain in all but three of Ian's 21 Tests.

'Until very recently, I would have said he was a better bowler than a batsman. I think his bowling has fallen off marginally in the last year. He doesn't get as high, doesn't swing the ball as much, or as often or as sharply – but then, he may be a bit tired. As for his batting, when I first saw him back in 1974, he seemed crude and a bit iffy. He still plays across the ball and at times tries to hit too many fours and sixes. But he's got such a marvellous eye, such marvellous timing and strength – and all the shots, really – that even if he stopped his bowling, hurt his ankle or somehow couldn't bowl, he would still be a Test batsman – without any question.

'As for his fielding, he is as good an all-round fielder as I've ever come across. He's good in the deep, and Randall and Gower don't field in the slips. In slips, he is the best I've ever fielded next to, except Tony Greig which, in my opinion, puts him on a par with Graham Roope. As a team player, he can be selfish – this irresponsibility in running out people, which happens because he gets carried away – but, over all, he has a certain generosity. In this respect, Ian's a sportsman and wholeheartedly accepts it when someone does better than he does – either in the opposition or the England side and probably Somerset, too.'

Botham was gone. He was due for dinner in Hove where Somerset, beginning the next day, were closing their championship season with a match against Sussex. It was a meaningless match. Essex already had won the title but with Richards, Rose and Garner being rested for the big week-end Botham was due to play. He loaded his gear into his car: clothes, cricket clobber, his Man of the Series award, the two generous telegrams and a nasty letter from a man on the Isle of Wight. It read: 'I have been following cricket for over 60 years and I have never seen such a selfish slob as you. All you think of is getting your name in the record book. I was so glad you got out at Leeds still needing three for your 1,000 runs. And as for that stupid headgear you wear. Poor little boy. Are you afraid of getting hurt? Didums, then, grow up and be a man.'

At Langford's Hotel in Hove, Botham was in the bar with Roebuck later that night when a man came up and asked for his autograph. Botham signed as he nearly always does. The man peered down at the signature, and said, 'Is that it?' Botham snapped back, 'Yes, that's it, mate. You can either take it or leave it.' He was tired and there was menace in his voice and when the man walked off Roebuck scolded his friend for being rude. 'Look,' said Botham, 'if you received some of the letters I get, you'd be rude to everybody.'

Over the next three days, Somerset lost the Sussex match by nine wickets, their only loss of the championship season. In cold print Botham's figures looked unexceptional: batting 40 and 15; bowling, no wickets and 102 runs from 30·1 overs. Statistics can lie. It was one of Botham's most interesting performances of the year. Somerset batted first, were all out for 322 (Botham 40), and Sussex came in at the fag end of the first day. Botham opened the bowling. Roebuck takes up the story:

'Both bowled three or four overs the first day and three or four the following morning, all quite quick but not really fast. Then he made an announcement: he was going to bowl his medium-paced "Tom Cartwright" stuff, and he went back about six paces and for the next hour and a quarter gave a beautiful demonstration of medium-paced bowling. I watched from first slip and it was beautiful. Swinging the ball both ways. No bouncers, no slow balls, no attempt at this or that, no impatience, no frustration that the game was going dead in his hands. I said, "Look Both, we've got a big game on Saturday, come off now." He said no, he was going to get this or that beggar out, and he kept bowling. It was an absurd situation: Dasher [Peter Denning, the acting captain] couldn't get him off. I couldn't get him off because you can't tell Botham to come off, you have to say please, which we did and finally he said OK, just a couple more overs and then, of course, he bowled about six maidens in succession. All together, he bowled about 25 overs without stopping.'

In fact, Botham's five maidens came during six overs but he did bowl 27 overs that innings, yielding up 86 runs without claiming a wicket. Sussex piled up runs off everyone and closed at 419. Somerset replied with an insufficient 232 (Botham 15) and the game was all but lost when Ian came back in the second Sussex innings to announce that he was an off-spinner. Roebuck again: 'He kept going on about how good an off-spinner he was, better than me, anyway, but not quite as good as Vic Marks. That's a joke. He's not bad but he's convinced he's slightly better than he is. Botham is always experimenting, but experimenting within a discipline.' Botham's off-spinners were limited to 3·1 overs during which he gave up 16 runs, before Sussex had won by nine wickets. Botham later confirmed the story although he didn't like the bit about his off-spin bowling being a 'joke'. He fancied himself an off-spinner and he put his case. 'If I walked into a side, completely new to the lads,' he said, 'and I said, "I bowl seamers and a little bit of off-spin," they automatically would say, "right", and give me a chance. Now, though, I have trouble getting through to the team. I'm convinced I can do it, now it's a matter of convincing others.' He brooded over the problem for a minute. 'If Mike Procter can bowl off-spin, why can't I?' It was the old festering wound: Procter bowling him out with that off-spin ball in 1976.

There is a time and a place for Botham off-spinning but one of them is not in the

Mike Procter, Gloucestershire and South Africa: 'If Procky can bowl off-spin,' asks Botham, 'why can't I?'

Gillette Cup final at Lord's, and on the morning after Hove he put aside his toy. The Somerset team sat over breakfast discussing the toss. Captain Rose had listened to the weather forecast: it would be fine and dry in the morning, getting cloudy in the afternoon, with the slight possibility of drizzle: in theory, Rose reasoned, Somerset should look to bat first on a dry wicket and bring on their bowling firepower under the cover of cloud. 'If we won the toss I was inclined to bat first,' recalled Rose, a captain who asks advice of his team, 'but Both and Garner didn't see it that way.'

Botham and Garner wanted the ball first. As strike bowlers in one-day matches, they were paralysing, especially Garner who in Somerset's three Gillette Cup matches that year had taken 11 wickets for only 63 runs. Rival captains tended to put Somerset in during limited-over matches to avoid first facing the wrath of Garner and Botham.

This, and the fact that the Gillette Cup final had been won since 1974 by the team batting second made the decision easy when Northamptonshire won the toss: their captain, Jim Watts, asked Somerset to bat. Rose and Denning, to the hysterical delight of coachloads of fans from the West Country, got away like the wind on an immaculate wicket and Richards, coming in after 34 runs, laid waste the Northamptonshire bowling. At 145 in the 39th over, Roebuck left, bringing Botham together with the fluent West Indian.

Botham later recalled the partnership. 'Northants brought their field in for me and left it out for Viv, which I took as a personal insult. Things were ticking over pretty well but we were losing overs and it came to the point where we had to start pushing the score along.' Botham and Richards met to consult in the middle. Botham cursed Watts for bringing the field in and he said he was fed up being shackled. He was going over the top. Richards agreed. Botham returned to the crease and exploded with the bat, racing his total past Richards'. In the Somerset President's box, Greg Chappell sat with Colin Atkinson, watching the match and discussing replacements Somerset might find for Richards and Garner when the two were on Test call for the West Indies. Chappell became engrossed with the onslaught from Botham.

'I get the feeling that Ian is more at ease in the England side than he is in the Somerset side,' the Australian captain said later. 'I think he feels equal to any England player, whereas, in the Gillette Cup final, he was trying to prove to himself, or to somebody, that he was as good a player as Viv Richards.' Once again an observer had seen Botham in competition with Richards. Botham finally was out, at 27, trying to slaughter a ball from Tim Lamb. It had been an electrifying partnership, worth 41 runs, and taking Somerset to 186 for four wickets. Richards went on and, using his bat with the delicacy of a surgeon, scored 117 and brought Somerset to 211 with eleven overs left. After some hiccups, the innings closed on 269 for eight. The omens seemed good and, as Rose had foreseen, clouds soon came drifting over Lord's. Garner and Botham set to work in fierce form. Botham bowled beautifully but without much luck. He played rather a sheet-anchor role to the gangling 6 ft 8 ins Garner who ripped mercilessly through the enemy ranks. Somerset's supporters sweated through a single sticky patch when Northamptonshire went from 12 to 137, but then the adroit Roebuck ran out the Northants opener, Geoff Cook, for the fourth wicket. Somerset fans began to chant out Northamptonshire's improbable run rate and the banners came up: 'Cider with Rosey' and 'Razor Sharp Somerset a Cut above Northants.'

Botham came on for his last spell. At this stage of a limited-over match it is his tactic to bowl to the leg stump, loading up the leg-side field. If he had his way, the leg-side

Gillette Cup celebrations! Somerset's captain Brian Rose, with Botham and Viv Richards, after winning the 1979 final and only a day before they did their double, capturing the John Player League.

load would be even heavier at such times. 'In the game of cricket there is one rule I would like to see changed,' he will say, 'the rule where you can have only two fielders behind square on the leg side. I'd like as many as I see fit.' The field he is forced to set is a deep fine leg, a backward square leg on the boundary, a man at mid-wicket, one at long-on and a couple filling in. 'Then I bowl it right up there in the block hole,' he will say, 'and they can't hit you very far.' There was little need for this at Lord's that day. Botham, returning to conventional line and length, bowled only ten of his dozen overs when Garner dismissed the tail and Northamptonshire were gone for 224 in 56.3 overs. Richards was adjudged Man of the Match and Garner, with six wickets for 29 runs, ran up his four-match 1979 Gillette Cup harvest to 17 wickets at 5·41 runs per wicket.

Grown men wept in the changing-room while, on the field below, a sea of Somerset supporters gathered to pay tribute to their team. Their cries rang out, wave upon wave, as they called for each of their heroes to appear on the balcony. Rose went out again and again, lifting the trophy as though it were bar-bells. Greg Chappell came in, happy and charmingly meek. A fusillade of champagne corks went off and Botham sprayed his mates with the ceremonial foam. He suddenly sat down and drank back a pitcher of beer. Somerset had won their first cricket title in 104 years and it was hard to believe. An hour later, Botham was driving with his team-mates Jennings and Breakwell towards Nottingham and it wasn't until they were in the hotel bar at 11 p.m. that a new fact hit them. There was more work to be done. Somerset were playing for a chance at another title, the John Player League, on the following day. 'We had had the best intentions of celebrating,' recalled Vic Marks, 'but somehow it didn't get off the ground. Our emotions were dead.'

These emotions didn't come alive again until well into the match on the following day. Nottingham, like Northamptonshire, shied away from the Somerset attack and upon winning the toss put Somerset in. Rose was bowled, attempting to drive, Denning was briefly useful and Richards, reckless after a day of care at Lord's, was bowled while making room to drive. In the 17th over, Somerset were 58 for the loss of three important wickets. The messages from Canterbury were equally grim: Middlesex, 47 for three, then 64 for four in the 20th over. Kent were on course to regain the John Player League championship. As he left the changing-room, bat flapping at his side, Botham was in an uncharacteristic mood. Somerset would lose, he reckoned, and so did others in the room. Rose called after him, goading and affectionate: 'How about some runs this time?'

The Nottinghamshire captain, Clive Rice, at that point made a crucial decision. With Roebuck and Botham now together, he took himself off. He had been bowling with chilling economy: six runs during five overs and the valued wicket of Denning. The studious Roebuck, playing what was to be his finest one-day innings, began to chip away at the change bowling and Botham began to butcher it. He hit two colossal leg-side sixes and, in two overs, he and Roebuck added 33 runs. The score now read: 103 runs for three wickets after 23 overs. He was not unaware of Kent's fortunes down at Canterbury. They came in shouts from the 2,000 Somerset fans, listening to transistor radios in the stands. Middlesex's middle-order batsmen, as though in response to Somerset, were staging a recovery: 106 for four wickets. 'We had left this match to chance,' Botham later recalled, 'and now, all of a sudden we could win it – and the League.'

Botham went on to score 30, Roebuck 50 and with Vic Marks picking up the slack, Somerset closed at 185 and immediately turned to news from Canterbury. Middlesex were all out for 182. There was ample room for optimism. Rose wheeled on his heavy artillery: Garner and Botham. They struck hard and fast. In the fourth over, Botham had the awkward-looking Basarat Hassan caught behind for 6, making Nottinghamshire 11 for one. Garner followed suit and Randall, prodding, was caught Taylor for 1, leaving Notts 15 for two. Botham's bowling continued admirably and in his opening spell of four overs he yielded only 14 runs, one boundary. Rose rung the changes and against Somerset's second-line attack the young Tim Robinson and especially Rice struck back, carrying Nottinghamshire into the 60s. The news from Canterbury was bleak: Kent, 41 for one. Nottinghamshire's third wicket didn't fall until 83 and, suddenly, they were 92 for five.

'All the time you would hear this tremendous uproar in the stand,' Marks recalled, 'and for no apparent reason. Then the message would get through. Another Kent wicket was gone.' Kent were 93 for five, beat for beat with Nottingham. Brearley was keeping his word to Botham. Nottinghamshire's end came quickly. Rose later remembered: 'When we had nine down, and Nottinghamshire had no chance of winning, we started putting a few close fielders in to finish them off. Then they hit a

John Player celebrations! Ian and his close friend and rival, Viv Richards, after the triumph at Nottingham.

The Bothams, at home in Epworth, South Humberside. Kathryn, Liam, Sarah, Ian and Tigger, the boxer dog.

couple of fours off Botham and we looked at each other. Knickers to this, there was going to be no trouble this time, and we put the field back.' Almost immediately, Bore was lbw to Botham and Ian, charging forward, ripped up a souvenir stump and fled to the pavilion. The chorus brought the news from Canterbury. Kent had lost. Somerset had won the John Player League championship.

Once again, champagne was poured in the changing-room and the players called, one by one, to be cheered on the balcony. It was over. The prevailing feeling among the players was one of relief and fatigue and none showed it more than Graham Burgess who had done his share when Somerset were cornered through the season. He was exhausted. He had had enough, he said, and after fourteen seasons with Somerset he was packing it in. Burgess pulled off his boots, tied the shoe-laces together and hobbled out onto the balcony where he draped them over one of the hanging flower baskets. The boots were still hanging there when the players set out for their homes.

The year 1979 had been a gratifying one for Ian Botham. It wasn't finished. In November he was named a selector for the England team that set out for a tour of Australia. In December he took eleven wickets in the Second Test against Australia and on the last day of the year, in a match against Queensland at Brisbane, he served as captain of England.

AFTERWORD

The Bells of Heaven: Australia and India, 1979–80

In school days the captaincy of a sports team goes, or ought to go, to the best player. And so it was some years ago in Yeovil when Botham, aged ten, led the Milford Junior School cricket team into battle. He was the youngest player in the team, yet he took command. 'He would get at one end and that was it,' remembers one of his team-mates of the day; 'he would bowl No. 1 and bat No. 1, but nobody minded. He knew what he was doing.'

Botham continued to captain his school teams but it wasn't until the Brisbane match at the end of 1979, England XI *v.* Queensland, that he again was out in the middle for the toss. He won it and, although under certain constraints, he knew what he wanted from his team: the outright effort he expects of himself. Tactically, Botham's main constraint had been imposed upon him by the selectors: team manager Alec Bedser, assistant team manager Barrington, captain Brearley, vice-captain Willis and himself. Needing rest after nearly eight weeks of touring, Botham was not to bowl. Once he had set his mind on this, much as he had set his mind on not hitting out in the crucial Ashes Test a year earlier in Sydney, he was content. 'I enjoyed it,' he said later. 'I had no temptation whatsoever to bowl at any stage of the match.'

His batting at Brisbane was clearly less of a success. Trying for a six, lamentably, he was out for twenty-one to a long hop from a leg-spinner. Barrington was worried: 'Ian had been trying to hit the ball too hard, sort out the Australians. Many times I told him, "Look, it would be one thing if you got twenty runs for hitting a ball 200 yards over the pavilion roof, but you don't, you get six. When you first go in, try to hit the ball back where it came from. Bend your left leg and have a look at what's going on. And concentrate." '

After the Queensland match, England faced Australia at Sydney; they were already one down in the series. The state of the ground was appalling, for the normally responsible curator, Athol Watkins, had neglected to cover the pitch three nights before the Test; it was left open to a Biblical deluge of rain. Brearley lost the toss. England were put in, and were all out for 123, with Botham top scorer with twenty-seven. As a bowler, Botham came to terms with the dud wicket. 'It was such a wet wicket,' he said later, 'that all you had to do was to run up and bowl line and length.' By this tidy expediency, he claimed four wickets in the first Australia innings of 145.

It was during England's reply of 237, on a drying wicket, that Ian's dismissal for a duck pin-pointed another of his batting problems. 'It was clear I was going too far over,

111

Black-padded batsman. Botham, while lusty, was less devastating in the World Series Cup matches. England beat Australia but lost the title to West Indies.

All-round satisfaction. Botham catches his bitter rival, Ian Chappell, off Derek Underwood, who reaches his 100th Australian Test wicket in the Sydney match.

Bouncer. Len Pascoe, who emerged from the series as Australia's one searingly fast bowler, alerts Botham at Melbourne. Botham helped in Somerset's unsuccessful pursuit of Pascoe.

almost toppling, when anything pitched middle or leg stump. I was playing round the ball and not with a straight bat, so I decided to change my guard from middle and leg to leg stump.' It was his key technical batting decision of the tour, one which would pay rich dividends.

England went on to lose the Sydney match by six wickets but, in Australia's second innings, Botham enjoyed a gratifying experience. Ian Chappell, who never forgot the indignity of being knocked off a bar stool by Botham, had mercilessly heckled the Englishman whenever he came to the crease on the tour. Botham seethed, held his tongue, but through the winter couldn't get Chappell out. His opportunity for a measure of reprisal came when, fielding close on the off side, he snapped up Chappell's blistering attacking shot off the bowling of Underwood. 'It was pure instinct,' recalled Botham, 'but it was quite a good catch.' It also was Underwood's 100th Australian wicket.

The Third Test at Melbourne, while resulting in Australia's third victory over England, was the most rewarding match of Botham's tour Down Under. His bat, as John Woodcock of *The Times* had predicted weeks before, 'rang like the bells of Heaven', and perhaps more importantly, Botham learned a lesson from the renegade Lillee. The Melbourne wicket was low and slow. 'A bloody awful wicket,' Botham thought upon first seeing it; 'it won't do anything with the seam.'

Batting first, England enjoyed their lustiest innings of the tour, 306 runs, thanks to Gooch's ninety-nine and Brearley's steadfast and unbeaten sixty. Botham got eight. In reply, Australia buried the visitors under a 477-run barrage, Greg Chappell scoring 114 and Botham generously yielding 105 runs for his three wickets. The England second innings began badly. Botham, dropping down the order, came in at ninety-two for six. But his new batting confidence, sharpened in the nets with Barrington, gave him the wisdom to make haste slowly and play each shot on its merit. At the end of the day, with Taylor holding up the other end, Botham had scored thirty runs and England had scrambled to 157. 'The ball kept low and, basically, I played every shot off the front foot,' Botham said; 'drives mostly, and straight down the ground.' The following morning he and Taylor had added eighty-six runs before the wicket-keeper, hooking rashly at a ball from Lillee, was caught: England, 178 for seven.

Botham scored 70 of the ninety-three runs that morning, hitting a variety of shots, but still chiefly hammering the straight drives with great gusto. His single bit of luck came at fifty-four when, pulling viciously at a ball from Lillee, he sent a rifle shot to deep square leg where Dymock, not the most skilful of fielders, spilled the catch. 'It wasn't a bad shot,' Botham said later, explaining away his mistake. 'There were two guys back there and I was just trying to help it round.' At the end of the England innings, Botham was still batting gloriously, 119 not out, England 273. As a batsman, Botham was back on song.

When he went out to bowl, he took as his model the new, slower Lillee who had destroyed England that day. In a fair facsimile of the Australian he bowled leg-cutters, off-cutters and in-swingers – and his figures tell a story of tight-reined discipline and skill – 12–5–18–1. England lost that Melbourne test by six wickets but Botham had regained his magic as a batsman and expanded his thinking as a bowler.

It was about at that time that Greg Chappell picked the best England team he had faced in his decade of Test cricket. It reads: Boycott, Edrich, Amiss, Woolmer, Gower, Illingworth (captain), Knott, Botham, Snow, Willis and Underwood, with the twelfth

The Heroes. Dennis Lillee, Player of the Australia–England Test Series, chats with Botham, England's star, in Bombay. Australia were en route to Tests in Pakistan.

India massacre. Botham, on the way to his 13 match wickets, has Sandeep Patil baffled by a lifting ball, caught behind in first innings at Bombay.

Gone. Botham, in firm form, smashing Ghavri to the boundary to make his hundredth run during his record-breaking 114 innings in the Bombay Jubilee Test.

man Hendrick. But for his batting, Chappell added, he would have selected Brearley to lead his mythical England side.

The final stop on the tour was Bombay where, on February 15, England joined India in the Golden Jubilee match in celebration of the fiftieth birthday of their Cricket Board of Control. The weather was hot, the air humid, the sun dazzling. Botham needed a new sun hat, size $7\frac{1}{2}$, and when none was to be found, Sunil Gavaskar, no stranger to floppy sun hats, sent a man to fetch one in the streets of Bombay.

It would be a long day. Despite the languid atmosphere, the most memorable one of all Botham's Tests.

India won the toss and batted. Lever and Botham opened the bowling. Gavaskar survived an early and confident Lever appeal and, unsettled began to attack recklessly. He hooked Lever high onto the pavilion for six, went on to smash eleven runs off Lever's second over, eleven off his third. Ian was surprised: Gavaskar is a man who plans to play himself in. Botham, his keenness rising, bowled sensibly, good line and length. He stuck mainly to his stock ball, the out-swinger that might lure Gavaskar into trouble. He was just settling in when, suddenly, he fell to Botham at forty-nine. 'I started a ball on the leg side and it swung a little,' Botham later recalled. 'He tried to sweep and he got a leading edge.' The ball climbed into the air. Taylor shouted 'mine' and the slip fielders dutifully fell back. The England wicket-keeper moved fifteen yards to take the catch. It was the first of Botham's thirteen wickets in the match, the first of Taylor's world-record ten catches.

India were now 102 for two. First ball after lunch, Vengsarkar fell to Graham Stevenson – the young Yorkshireman's first Test victim. The esteemed Viswanath was bowled by Lever: India 135 for four. Botham returned, full of fire. In a single over he got both Sandeep Patil, caught behind, and Kapil Dev with balls that swung and lifted.

On a softening pitch, Botham was to take three more wickets that day – and finish the day with six wickets at the cost of only fifty-eight runs. For the thirteenth time in only twenty-five Tests, he had taken five or more wickets in an innings. As for Taylor, with seven catches, he had equalled a world innings record set by the Pakistani, Wasim Bari. India were all out for 242.

Rest Day was taken on the second day, owing to a total solar eclipse, but for Botham there was no rest. In the team's luxurious Taj Mahal hotel, where he roomed with Underwood, the telephone never stopped ringing. Idolatrous fans wanted a word with the great 'Mr Iron Bottom', as they nearly pronounced it. 'The number of phone calls was amazing,' recalled Chris Lander of the *Daily Mirror* who was there to write columns with Underwood. 'Ian finally employed us as secretaries.' One man drove for miles with his family, bearing a garland of flowers. He came with a photographer in tow to Mr Iron Bottom's room. 'I have been photographed with the great Dexter and Barrington,' he said and, draping the flowers round Ian's neck, posed for a picture in the hotel corridor. At a reception, an Indian cricket official spoke to Underwood about the posters round Bombay that heralded the recent visit of Muhammad Ali. 'They have got it wrong,' he said, 'Mr Iron Bottom is the Greatest.' And all credit to Ian: through all this his cap size remained at $7\frac{1}{2}$ and, furthermore, he would be the last man to retell these stories.

The following day England's top order batsmen slumped. Botham came in at fifty-seven for four. As he had done since Sydney, he took a leg-stump guard. As he had done since Melbourne, he played himself in; blocking out, content to wait for the bad

Taylor's record. England's 'keeper, diving, catches Shivlal Yadav off a loosener from Botham to claim his tenth catch in the Jubilee match, a world record.

The end. Botham, after his debut with Scunthorpe United football reserves, only days after his return from the exhausting 1979–80 cricket tour of Australia and India. He later signed papers and played as an amateur in a first-team game for Scunthorpe against Bournemouth.

117

ball. Taylor, who in the past couple dozen Tests had often batted in partnership with Botham, noticed that Ian was in a 'correct mood'. Botham began scoring. 'He times the ball so well. He's so strong and the outfield was so quick,' Taylor later recalled, 'that all he had to do was block and he had a boundary.' His sixth-wicket partnership with Botham was to add 171 runs, a record for England against India, and steer England towards victory.

Botham was the senior partner. In 206 minutes, he played a powerful but measured innings and with seventeen boundaries and no sixes scored his second successive century. Basically, his runs came square of the wicket. He made only one error when, on ninety-six, he attempted to sweep Doshi and got a top edge. The ball just cleared the upstretched fingers of Kapil Dev.

He reached his century next over when he square-drove a full length ball from Ghavri, wide of the off stump, to the boundary. With that shot, Botham became the first man to have taken five wickets and scored a century in the same Test three times.

When he was 114 and England 229, thirteen runs short of the India first innings total, Botham lost his wicket. 'Ghavri bowled a delivery that started outside the off stump, came in quite late and nipped off the wicket and onto me.' He was trapped, leg before. At the end of the day, England were 232 for six. Botham, out for 114, had played imperiously well. 'That was,' said Barrington, 'the most mature innings I ever saw Ian play.' England were all out for 296, a lead of fifty-four.

Botham came on to bowl just before lunch, and was to bowl unchanged until stumps. With his third ball, he had Binny leg before. Viswanath went next. Botham got him leg before with his stock ball, an out-swinger. Botham also had Patil lbw next ball.

He didn't get his first Test hat-trick. But he soon got his ninth wicket. Gavaskar, caught Taylor for twenty-four. India were fifty-six for five, and in retreat. Kirmani was caught Gooch, bowled Botham for a duck. India: fifty-eight for six. Yashpal Sharma, given leg before, soon brought Ian another Test record. He now had a century and twelve wickets in a Test, surpassing the hundred runs (forty-four and eighty) and eleven wickets achieved by the Australian Alan Davidson against West Indies at Brisbane in 1960–61.

The day ended with India 148 for eight and next morning Botham and Taylor lost no time in setting yet another record. Off the very first ball of the day, a loosener, Yadav nicked a chance to Taylor who took it diving forward to his right. It was Taylor's tenth catch of the match, breaking the record (eight catches and a stumping) set at Lord's in 1956 by Gil Langley of Australia. Botham's thirteenth wicket of the match. India's last wicket, Doshi's, fell to Lever and their innings ended at 149. England,needing ninety-six to win, made short work of it and won the Jubilee Test match by ten wickets.

Botham's bowling figures at Bombay were 45.5–14–106–13. 'It was by far the most hostile and intelligent performance I have seen by an England bowler since the days of Trueman and Statham,' said Barrington. Brearley passed along praise to be treasured. 'I have seen only one person to compare with Botham,' he said, 'and that is Gary Sobers.' As for Botham himself, he celebrated the evening by dining in his room – on Indian food.

APPENDIX

I.T. BOTHAM — TEST MATCHES

DATE	FOR	OPPONENTS	VENUE	N°	RUNS	HOW OUT	NWS	BALLS	6s	4s	O	M	R	W	C	St	R	Notes
JUL 28 AUG 2	ENGLAND	AUSTRALIA (3)	N'ham	8	25	b		93	61		3	20	5	74	5	1		W	TEST DEBUT aged 21 yrs days. 5w/1
11-15	"	(4)	Leeds	8	0	l.b.w-Bright			3		·	25	5	60		·		W	Fractured bone in left foot - missed 5th TEST. 5w/2
FEB 10-15		N.Z. (1)	Wellington	7	7	c					·	12⁴	2	27	2	1		L	
				6	19	c					·	9³	3	13	2				
24 MAR 1	"	(2)	Christchurch	7	103	c wkt					·	24⁷	6	73	5	·		W	(1) 5w/3 HUNDRED and 5w/ins - 2nd instance by ENG in Tests (AW GREIG in 1973-4 WI)
				4	30	n.o.						7	1	38	3	3			
4-10	"	(3)	Auckland	6	53	c wkt					·	34	4	109	5	·		D	5w/4
											13	1	51		·			
JUN 1-5	PAKISTAN (1)		B'ham	7	100	c		195	140		11	15	4	52	1	1		W	(2) 122(66). G. MILLER
											17	3	47		·			
15-19	"	(2)	Lord's	7	108	b		166	110		12	5	2	17		·		W	(3) 118(6th) G.R.J. Roope. 100 off 104 balls in 157 minutes. 5w/5 BB FIRST TO SCORE 100 AND TAKE 8w IN SAME TEST. RECORD ANAL. in
											20⁵	8	34	8	1			
29 JUL 4	"	(3)	Leeds	8	4	lbw		7	6		·	18	2	59	4	1		D	TESTS AT LORD'S and E.V.P.
AUG 1		N.Z. (1)	Oval	7	22	c		80	80		2	22	7	58	1	·		W	
											19	2	46	3	·			
10-14	"	(2)	N'ham	6	8	c		9	16		·	21	9	34	6	·		W	5w/6 50 WKTS
											24	7	59	3	2			
24-28	"	(3)	Lord's	6	21	c wkt		96	78		3	38	13	101	6	·		W	5w/7
											18¹	4	39	5	·			5w/8 10w/1 (11-140)
DEC 1-6		AUSTRALIA (1)	Brisbane	7	49	c wkt		102	73		5	12	1	40	3	·		W	
											26	5	95	3	·			
15-20	"	(2)	Perth	6	11	lbw		44	28		1	11	2	46		1		W	
				6	30	c		52	39		4	11	1	54		·			
29 JAN 3	"	(3)	Melbourne	6	22	c		83	80		3	20⁴	4	68	3	·		L	
				6	10	c wkt		76	62		·	15	4	41	3	·			
6-11	"	(4)	Sydney	7	59	c wkt		138	108		7	28	3	87	2	3		W	
				6	90	b		90	88		·					·			
27 FEB 1	"	(5)	Adelaide	6	74	c wkt		158	97	2	6	11⁴	0	42	4	·		W	
				6	7	c		30	29		1	14⁴	4	37	1	·			(Wm Darling) on Jan 11
10-14	"	(6)	Sydney	6	23	c		54	53		2	9¹	1	57	4	2		W	Batted suffering from headache, virus & high temp. Hit on helmet at short leg
															2			
JUL 12-16		INDIA (1)	B'ham	6	33	b		33	39	1	4	26	4	86	2	3		W	5w/9
											29	8	70	5	1			
AUG 2-7	"	(2)	Lord's	6	36	b		74	63		3	19	9	35	5	1		D	5w/10
											35	13	80	1	·			100 wkts (S.M.Gavaskar ct Brearley on AUG 6). RECORD TIME OF 2yrs 9 days.
16-21	"	(3)	Leeds	6	137	c		201	152	5	16	13	3	39		·		D	(4) HS Scored 99* before lunch 4th day (9*-108*) EQUALLED RECORD FOR MOST SIXES IN A TEST IN ENGLAND. 100 in 170 minutes off 121 balls.
30 SEP 4	"	(4)	Oval	6	38	st		52	55	1	4	28	7	65	4	2		D	1000 RUNS (WHEN 3*) COMPLETED 'DOUBLE' IN 21 TESTS-RECORD.
				6	0	Ro		4	3		·	29	5	97	3	2			
DEC 14-19	AUSTRALIA (1)		Perth	7	15	c		17	16		2	35	9	78	6	·		L	5w/11
				6	18	c wkt		70	44		3	45³	14	98	5	·			
JAN 4-8	"	(2)	Sydney	7	27	c		27	22	1	1	17	7	29	4	·		L	5w/12 10w/2 (11-176)
				8	0	c		20	20		1	23³	12	43		1			
FEB 1-6	"	(3)	Melbourne	8	8	c wkt		29	21		1	39³	15	105	3	2		L	
				6	119	n.o.		224	213	1	15	12	5	18	1	·			
FEB 15-19		INDIA (1)	Bombay	6	114	lbw		206	144		17	22³	7	58	6	·		W	(5) 5w/13 (6) 171 (6th) R.W.Taylor — ENG v INDIA record. 5w/14 10w/3 (13-106) UNIQUE MATCH DOUBLE record match analysis v INDIA
											26	7	48	7	·			

SOMERSET v. NORTHAMPTONSHIRE
GILLETTE CUP FINAL
At Lord's, September 8, 1979

SOMERSET

*B. C. Rose b Watts	41
P. W. Denning c Sharp b Sarfraz	19
I. V. A. Richards b Griffiths	117
P. M. Roebuck b Willey	14
I. T. Botham b T. M. Lamb	27
V. J. Marks b Griffiths	9
G. I. Burgess c Sharp b Watts	1
D. Breakwell b T. M. Lamb	5
J. Garner not out	24
†D. J. S. Taylor not out	1
B 5, l-b 3, n-b 3	11
(8 wkts)	269

1/34 2/95 3/145 4/186
5/213 6/214 7/219 8/268

K. F. Jennings did not bat.

Bowling: Sarfraz 12–3–51–1; Griffiths 12–1–58–2; Watts 12–2–34–2; T. M. Lamb 12–0–70–2; Willey 12–2–45–1.

NORTHAMPTONSHIRE

G. Cook run out	44
W. Larkins lbw b Garner	0
R. G. Williams ht wkt b Garner	8
A. J. Lamb st Taylor b Richards	78
P. Willey c Taylor b Garner	5
T. J. Yardley c Richards b Burgess	20
†G. Sharp b Garner	22
Sarfraz Nawaz not out	16
T. M. Lamb b Garner	4
B. J. Griffiths b Garner	0
*P. J. Watts absent hurt.	
B 6, l-b 9, w 5, n-b 7	27
	224

1/3 2/13 3/126 4/138 5/170
6/186 7/218 8/224 9/224

Bowling: Garner 10.3–3–29–6; Botham 10–3–27–0; Jennings 12–1–29–0; Burgess 9–1–37–1; Marks 4–0–22–0; Richards 9–0–44–1; Breakwell 2–0–9–0.

Umpires: D. J. Constant and J. G. Langridge.

Somerset won by 45 runs.

NOTTINGHAMSHIRE v. SOMERSET
JOHN PLAYER LEAGUE
At Nottingham, September 9, 1979

SOMERSET

*B. C. Rose b Watson	4
P. W. Denning b Rice	21
I. V. A. Richards b Hemmings	25
P. M. Roebuck c Birch b Watson	50
I. T. Botham c Birch b Hemmings	30
G. I. Burgess b Bore	6
V. J. Marks c Randall b Cooper	14
J. Garner c and b Rice	0
D. Breakwell not out	8
C. H. Dredge not out	2
B 8, l-b 15, n-b 2	25
(8 wkts)	135

1/10 2/56 3/58 4/114 5/131
6/166 7/168 8/182

†D. J. S. Taylor did not bat.

Bowling: Watson 8–0–27–2; Bore 8–2–18–1; Hemmings 8–0–43–2; Cooper 7–0–55–1; Rice 7–2–13–2; Tunnicliffe 1–0–4–0.

NOTTINGHAMSHIRE

B. Hassan c Taylor b Botham	6
R. T. Robinson run out	35
D. W. Randall c Taylor b Garner	1
*C. E. B. Rice lbw b Dredge	39
J. D. Birch lbw b Dredge	2
H. T. Tunnicliffe c Taylor b Burgess	5
†M. J. Harris not out	17
E. E. Hemmings b Richards	0
W. K. Watson c Taylor b Garner	5
K. Cooper b Garner	0
M. K. Bore lbw b Botham	7
L-b 5, w 3, n-b 4	12
	129

1/11 2/15 3/83 4/91 5/96
6/99 7/102 8/119 9/119

Bowling: Garner 6–2–16–3; Botham 5.1–0–18–2; Dredge 8–2–28–2; Burgess 7–0–40–1; Richard 7–1–15–1.

Umpires: R. Julian and J. Van Geloven.

Somerset won by 56 runs.

ENGLAND v. AUSTRALIA
THIRD TEST MATCH
At Nottingham, July 28, 29, 30, August 1, 2, 1977

AUSTRALIA

R. B. McCosker c Brearley b Hendrick	51	c Brearley b Willis	107
I. C. Davis c Botham b Underwood	33	c Greig b Willis	9
*G. S. Chappell b Botham	19	b Hendrick	27
D. W. Hookes c Hendrick b Willis	17	lbw b Hendrick	42
K. D. Walters c Hendrick b Botham	11	c Randall b Greig	28
R. D. Robinson c Brearley b Greig	11	lbw b Underwood	34
†R. W. Marsh lbw b Botham	0	c Greig b Willis	0
K. J. O'Keeffe not out	48	not out	21
M. H. N. Walker c Hendrick b Botham	0	b Willis	17
J. R. Thomson b Botham	21	b Willis	0
L. S. Pascoe c Greig b Hendrick	20	c Hendrick b Underwood	0
B 4, l-b 2, n-b 6	12	B 1, l-b 5, w 1, n-b 17	24
	243		309

1/79 2/101 3/131 4/133
5/153 6/153 7/153 8/155 9/196

1/18 2/60 3/154 4/204
5/240 6/240 7/270 8/307 9/308

Bowling: *First Innings*—Willis 15-0-58-1; Hendrick 21.2-6-46-2; Botham 20-5-74-5; Greig 15-4-35-1; Underwood 11-5-18-1. *Second Innings*—Willis 26-6-88-5; Hendrick 32-14-56-2; Botham 25-5-60-0; Greig 9-2-24-1; Underwood 27-15-49-2; Miller 5-2-5-0; Woolmer 3-0-3-0.

ENGLAND

*J. M. Brearley c Hookes b Pascoe	15	b Walker	81
G. Boycott c McCosker b Thomson	107	not out	80
R. A. Woolmer lbw b Pascoe	0		
D. W. Randall run out	13	not out	19
A. W. Greig b Thomson	11	b Walker	0
G. Miller c Robinson b Pascoe	13		
†A. P. E. Knott c Davis b Thomson	135	c O'Keeffe b Walker	2
I. T. Botham b Walker	25		
D. L. Underwood b Pascoe	7		
M. Hendrick b Walker	1		
R. G. D. Willis not out	2		
B 9, l-b 7, w 3, n-b 16	35	B 2, l-b 2, w 1, n-b 2	7
	364	(3 wkts)	189

1/34 2/34 3/52 4/64
5/82 6/297 7/326 8/357 9/357

1/154 2/156 3/158

Bowling: *First Innings*—Thomson 31-6-103-3; Pascoe 32-10-80-4; Walker 39.2-12-79-2; Chappell 8-0-19-0; O'Keeffe 11-4-43-0; Walters 3-0-5-0. *Second Innings*—Thomson 16-6-34-0; Pascoe 22-6-43-0; O'Keeffe 19.2-6-65-0; Walker 24-8-40-3.

England won by seven wickets.

Umpires: H. D. Bird and D. J. Constant.

ENGLAND v. AUSTRALIA
FOURTH TEST MATCH
At Leeds, August 11, 12, 13, 15, 1977

ENGLAND

*J. M. Brearley c Marsh b Thomson	0
G. Boycott c Chappell b Pascoe	191
R. A. Woolmer c Chappell b Thomson	37
D. W. Randall lbw b Pascoe	20
A. W. Greig b Thomson	43
G. R. J. Roope c Walters b Thomson	34
†A. P. E. Knott lbw b Bright	57
I. T. Botham b Bright	0
D. L. Underwood c Bright b Pascoe	6
M. Hendrick c Robinson b Pascoe	4
R. G. D. Willis not out	5
B 5, l-b 9, w 3, n-b 22	39
	436

1/0 2/82 3/105 4/201
5/275 6/398 7/398 8/412 9/422

Bowling: Thomson 34-7-113-4; Walker 48-21-97-0; Pascoe 34.4-10-19-4; Walters 3-1-5-0; Bright 26-9-66-2; Chappell 10-2-25-0.

AUSTRALIA

R. B. McCosker run out	27	c Knott b Greig	12
I. C. Davis lbw b Hendrick	0	c Knott b Greig	19
*G. S. Chappell c Brearley b Hendrick	4	c Greig b Willis	36
D. W. Hookes lbw b Botham	24	lbw b Hendrick	21
K. D. Walters c Hendrick b Botham	4	lbw b Woolmer	15
R. D. Robinson c Greig b Hendrick	20	b Hendrick	20
†R. W. Marsh c Knott b Botham	2	c Randall b Hendrick	63
R. J. Bright not out	9	c Greig b Hendrick	5
M. H. N. Walker c Knott b Botham	7	b Willis	30
J. R. Thomson b Botham	0	b Willis	0
L. S. Pascoe b Hendrick	0	not out	0
L-b 3, w 1, n-b 2	6	B 1, l-b 4, w 4, n-b 18	27
	103		248

1/8 2/26 3/52 4/57
5/66 6/77 7/87 8/100 9/100

1/31 2/35 3/63 4/97
5/130 6/167 7/179 8/244 9/245

Bowling: *First Innings*—Willis 5-0-35-0; Hendrick 15.3-2-41-4; Botham 11-3-21-5. *Second Innings*—Willis 14-7-32-3; Hendrick 22.5-6-54-4; Greig 20-7-64-2; Botham 17-3-47-0; Woolmer 8-4-8-1; Underwood 8-3-16-0.

Umpires: W. L. Budd and W. E. Alley.

England won by an innings and 85 runs.

NEW ZEALAND v. ENGLAND
FIRST TEST MATCH
At Wellington, February 10, 11, 12, 14, 15, 1978

NEW ZEALAND

Batsman	First Innings		Second Innings	
R. W. Anderson	c Taylor b Old	28	lbw b Old	26
J. G. Wright	lbw b Botham	55	c Roope b Willis	21
G. P. Howarth	c Botham b Old	13	c Edmonds b Willis	22
*M. G. Burgess	b Willis	9	c Boycott b Botham	6
B. E. Congdon	c Taylor b Old	44	c Roope b Willis	0
J. M. Parker	c Rose b Willis	16	c Edmonds b Willis	4
†W. K. Lees	c Taylor b Old	1	lbw b Hendrick	11
R. J. Hadlee	not out	27	c Boycott b Willis	2
D. R. Hadlee	c Taylor b Old	1	c Edmonds b Botham	2
R. O. Collinge	b Old	4	c Edmonds b Hendrick	3
S. L. Boock	b Botham	0	not out	0
Extras	B 12, l-b 3, w 1, n-b 13	29	B 3, l-b 8, w 2, n-b 13	26
Total		**228**		**123**

1/42 2/96 3/114 4/152 5/191 6/193 7/194 8/196 9/208

1/54 2/82 3/93 4/93 5/98 6/99 7/104 8/116 9/123

Bowling: *First Innings*—Willis 25-7-65-2; Hendrick 17-2-46-0; Old 30-11-54-6; Edmonds 3-1-7-0; Botham 12.6-2-27-2. *Second Innings*—Willis 15-2-32-5; Hendrick 10-2-16-2; Old 9-2-32-1; Edmonds 1-0-4-0; Botham 9.3-3-13-2.

ENGLAND

Batsman	First Innings		Second Innings	
B. C. Rose	c Lees b Collinge	21	not out	5
*G. Boycott	c Congdon b Collinge	77	b Collinge	1
G. Miller	b Boock	24	c Anderson b Collinge	4
†R. W. Taylor	c and b Collinge	8	run out	0
D. W. Randall	c Burgess b R. Hadlee	4	lbw b Collinge	9
G. R. J. Roope	c Lees b R. Hadlee	37	c Lees b R. Hadlee	0
I. T. Botham	c Burgess b R. Hadlee	7	c Boock b R. Hadlee	19
C. M. Old	b R. Hadlee	10	lbw b R. Hadlee	9
P. H. Edmonds	lbw b Congdon	4	c Parker b R. Hadlee	11
M. Hendrick	lbw b Congdon	0	c Parker b R. Hadlee	0
R. G. D. Willis	not out	6	c Howarth b R. Hadlee	3
Extras	B 1, l-b 3, n-b 13	17	N-b 3	3
Total		**215**		**64**

1/39 2/89 3/108 4/126 5/183 6/188 7/203 8/205 9/205

1/2 2/8 3/18 4/18 5/38 6/38 7/53 8/53 9/63

Bowling: *First Innings*—R. Hadlee 28-5-74-4; Congdon 17.4-11-14-2; Collinge 18-5-42-3; D. Hadlee 21-5-47-0; Boock 10-5-21-1. *Second Innings*—R. Hadlee 13.3-4-26-6; Collinge 13-5-35-3; D. Hadlee 1-1-0-0.

Umpires: W. R. C. Gardiner and R. L. Monteith.

New Zealand won by 72 runs.

NEW ZEALAND v. ENGLAND
SECOND TEST MATCH
At Christchurch, February 24, 25, 26, 28, March 1, 1978

ENGLAND

Batsman	First Innings		Second Innings	
B. C. Rose	c Howarth b Chatfield	11	c Lees b Collinge	7
*G. Boycott	lbw b Collinge	8	run out	26
D. W. Randall	c Burgess b Hadlee	0	run out	13
G. R. J. Roope	c Burgess b Hadlee	50	not out	9
G. Miller	c Congdon b Collinge	89		
C. T. Radley	c Lees b Hadlee	15		
I. T. Botham	c Lees b Boock	103	not out	30
†R. W. Taylor	run out	45		
C. M. Old	b Hadlee	8		
P. H. Edmonds	c Lees b Collinge	50	b Collinge	1
R. G. D. Willis	not out	6		
Extras	B 14, l-b 9, n-b 10	33	B 4, l-b 3, n-b 3	10
Total		**418**	(4 wkts dec.)	**96**

1/15 2/18 3/26 4/127 5/128 6/288 7/293 8/305 9/375

1/25 2/47 3/67 4/74

Bowling: *First Innings*—Hadlee 43-10-147-4; Collinge 26.5-6-89-3; Chatfield 37-8-94-1; Congdon 18-11-14-0; Boock 21-11-41-1. *Second Innings*—Hadlee 6-1-17-0; Collinge 9-2-29-2; Chatfield 5-0-22-0; Congdon 2-0-18-0.

NEW ZEALAND

Batsman	First Innings		Second Innings	
J. G. Wright	c and b Edmonds	4	c Roope b Willis	0
R. W. Anderson	b Edmonds	62	b Willis	15
G. P. Howarth	c Edmonds b Willis	5	c Edmonds b Old	1
*M. G. Burgess	c Roope b Botham	29	not out	6
B. E. Congdon	lbw b Botham	20	c Botham b Willis	0
J. M. Parker	not out	53	c Botham b Edmonds	16
†W. K. Lees	c Miller b Botham	0	b Willis	0
R. J. Hadlee	b Edmonds	1	c Botham b Edmonds	39
R. O. Collinge	c Edmonds b Botham	32	c Miller b Botham	0
S. L. Boock	c Taylor b Edmonds	2	c Taylor b Botham	0
E. J. Chatfield	c Edmonds b Botham	3	lbw b Botham	6
Extras	B 4, l-b 1, n-b 19	24	L-b 6, n-b 16	22
Total		**235**		**105**

1/37 2/52 3/82 4/119 5/148 6/151 7/153 8/211 9/216

1/2 2/14 3/19 4/25 5/25 6/59 7/81 8/90 9/95

Bowling: *First Innings*—Willis 20-1-45-1; Old 14-4-55-0; Botham 24.7-6-73-5; Edmonds 34-10-38-4. *Second Innings*—Willis 7-2-14-4; Old 7-4-9-1; Botham 7-1-38-3; Edmonds 6-2-22-2.

Umpires: F. R. Goodall and R. L. Monteith.

England won by 174 runs.

NEW ZEALAND v. ENGLAND
THIRD TEST MATCH
At Auckland, March 4, 5, 6, 8, 9, 10, 1978

NEW ZEALAND

Batsman	First Innings		Second Innings	
J. G. Wright	c Taylor b Lever	4	c Taylor b Edmonds	25
R. W. Anderson	c Gatting b Botham	17	c Botham b Miller	55
G. P. Howarth	c Roope b Willis	122	b Miller	102
*M. G. Burgess	c Randall b Botham	50	c Taylor b Edmonds	17
B. E. Congdon	c Miller b Botham	5	c Roope b Lever	20
J. M. Parker	lbw b Botham	14	not out	47
†G. N. Edwards	lbw b Lever	55	c Randall b Lever	54
R. J. Hadlee	c Roope b Botham	1	b Miller	10
B. L. Cairns	b Lever	11	lbw b Edmonds	20
R. O. Collinge	not out	5	not out	12
S. L. Boock	c Edmonds b Willis	1		
Extras	B 5, l-b 10, n-b 15	30	B 6, l-b 4, n-b 10	20
Total		315	(8 wkts)	382

1/12 2/32 3/113 4/129 5/182 6/278 7/285 8/302 9/314

1/69 2/98 3/125 4/185 5/272 6/287 7/305 8/350

Bowling: *First Innings*—Willis 26.6–8–57–2; Lever 34–5–96–3; Botham 34–4–109–5; Edmonds 10–2–23–0; Miller 1–1–0–0. *Second Innings*—Willis 10–3–42–0; Lever 17–4–59–2; Botham 13–1–51–0; Edmonds 45–15–107–3; Miller 30–10–99–3; Gatting 1–0–1–0; Roope 1–0–2–0; Randall 1–0–1–0.

ENGLAND

*G. Boycott	c Burgess b Collinge	54
D. W. Randall	lbw b Hadlee	30
C. T. Radley	c Wright b Collinge	158
G. R. J. Roope	c Burgess b Boock	68
M. W. Gatting	b Boock	0
I. T. Botham	c Edwards b Collinge	53
†R. W. Taylor	b Boock	16
G. Miller	lbw b Collinge	15
P. H. Edmonds	b Boock	8
J. K. Lever	c and b Boock	1
R. G. D. Willis	not out	0
Extras	B 6, l-b 6, 24, n-b 10	26
Total		429

1/52 2/115 3/254 4/258 5/355 6/396 7/418 8/427 9/428

Bowling: Hadlee 31–6–107–1; Collinge 38–9–98–4; Cairns 33–9–63–0; Congdon 26–8–68–0; Boock 28.3–4–67–5.

Umpires: W. R. C. Gardiner and J. B. R. Hastie.

Match drawn.

ENGLAND v. PAKISTAN
FIRST CORNHILL TEST
At Birmingham, June 1, 2, 3, 5, 1978

PAKISTAN

Batsman	First Innings		Second Innings	
Mudassar Nazar	c and b Botham	14	b Edmonds	30
Sadiq Mohammad	c Radley b Old	23	b Old	79
Mohsin Khan	b Willis	35	c Old b Miller	38
Javed Miandad	c Taylor b Old	15	c Brearley b Edmonds	39
Haroon Rashid	c Roope b Willis	3	b Willis	4
Wasim Raja	c Taylor b Old	17	b Edmonds	9
Sarfraz Nawaz	not out	32	not out	6
*†Wasim Bari	b Old	0	c Miller b Edmonds	3
Iqbal Qasim	c Taylor b Old	0	retired hurt	5
Sikander Bakht	c Roope b Old	0	c Roope b Miller	2
Liaqat Ali	c Brearley b Old	9	b Willis	3
Extras	L-b 3, n-b 13	16	B 4, l-b 4, w 1, n-b 4	13
Total		164		231

1/20 2/56 3/91 4/94 5/103 6/125 7/125 8/126 9/126

1/94 2/123 3/176 4/193 5/214 6/220 7/224 8/227 9/231

Bowling: *First Innings*—Willis 16–2–42–2; Old 22.4–6–50–7 Botham 15–4–52–1; Wood 3–2–2–0; Edmonds 4–2–2–0. *Second Innings*—Willis 23.4–3–70–2; Old 25–12–38–1; Botham 17–3–47–0; Edmonds 26–10–44–4; Miller 12–4–19–2.

ENGLAND

*J. M. Brearley	run out	38
B. Wood	lbw b Sikander	14
C. T. Radley	lbw b Sikander	106
D. I. Gower	c Miandad b Sikander	58
G. R. J. Roope	b Sikander	32
G. Miller	c Bari b Mudassar	48
I. T. Botham	c Qasim b Liaqat	100
C. M. Old	c Mudassar b Qasim	5
P. H. Edmonds	not out	4
Extras	L-b 26, w 5, n-b 16	46
Total	(8 wkts dec.)	452

1/36 2/101 3/190 4/275 5/276 6/399 7/447 8/452

†R. W. Taylor and R. G. D. Willis did not bat.

Bowling: Sarfraz 6–1–12–0; Liaqat 42–9–114–1; Mudassar 27–7–59–1; Qasim 14–2–56–1; Sikander 45–13–132–4; Raja 10–1–32–0.

Umpires: H. D. Bird and K. E. Palmer.

England won by an innings and 57 runs.

ENGLAND

*J. M. Brearley lbw b Liaqat	2
G. A. Gooch lbw b Raja	54
C. T. Radley c Mohsin b Liaqat	8
D. I. Gower b Qasim	56
G. R. J. Roope c Mohsin b Qasim	69
G. Miller c Miandad b Qasim	0
I. T. Botham b Liaqat	108
†R. W. Taylor c Mudassar b Sikander	10
C. M. Old c Mohsin b Sikander	0
P. H. Edmonds not out	36
R. G. D. Willis b Mudassar	18
L-b 2, n-b 1	3
	364

1/5 2/19 3/120 4/120 5/134
6/252 7/290 8/290 9/324

Bowling: Sikander 27–3–115–2; Liaqat 18–1–80–3; Mudassar 4.2–0–16–1; Qasim 30–5–101–3; Raja 12–3–49–1.

PAKISTAN

Sadiq Mohammad c Botham b Willis	11	c Taylor b Willis	0
Mudassar Nazar c Edmonds by Willis	1	c Taylor b Botham	10
Mohsin Khan c Willis b Edmonds	31	c Roope b Willis	46
Haroon Rashid b Old	15	b Botham	4
Javed Miandad c Taylor b Willis	0	c Gooch b Botham	22
Wasim Raja b Edmonds	28	c and b Botham	1
Talat Ali c Radley b Edmonds	2	c Roope b Botham	40
*Wasim Bari c Brearley b Willis	0	c Taylor b Botham	2
Iqbal Qasim b Willis	0	b Botham	0
Sikander Bakht c Brearley b Edmonds	4	c Roope b Botham	1
Liaqat Ali not out	4	not out	0
N-b 9	9	B 1, l-b 3, w 5, n-b 4	13
	105		139

1/11 2/22 3/40 4/41 5/84
6/96 7/97 8/97 9/97

1/1 2/45 3/100 4/108 5/114
6/119 7/121 8/130 9/130

Bowling: *First Innings*—Willis 13–1–47–5; Old 10–3–26–1; Botham 5–2–17–0; Edmonds 8–6–6–4. *Second Innings*—Willis 10–2–26–2; Old 15–4–36–0; Botham 20.5–8–34–8; Edmonds 12–4–21–0; Miller 9–3–9–0.

Umpires: W. L. Budd and D. J. Constant.

England won by an innings and 120 runs.

PAKISTAN

Sadiq Mohammad c Brearley b Botham	97
Mudassar Nazar c Botham b Old	31
Mohsin Khan lbw b Willis	41
Talat Ali c Gooch b Willis	0
Haroon Rashid c Brearley b Botham	7
Javed Miandad b Old	1
Wasim Raja lbw b Botham	0
Sarfraz Nawaz c Taylor b Botham	4
Sikander Bakht b Old	4
*†Wasim Bari not out	7
Iqbal Qasim lbw b Old	0
L-b 8, n-b 1	9
	201

1/75 2/147 3/147 4/169 5/182
6/183 7/189 8/190 9/201

Bowling: Willis 26–8–48–2; Old 41.4–22–41–4; Botham 18–2–59–4; Edmonds 11–2–22–0; Miller 9–3–22–0.

ENGLAND

*J. M. Brearley c Bari b Sarfraz	0
G. A. Gooch lbw b Sarfraz	20
C. T. Radley b Sikander	7
D. I. Gower lbw b Sarfraz	39
G. R. J. Roope c Sadiq b Miandad	11
G. Miller not out	18
†R. W. Taylor c Bari b Sarfraz	2
I. T. Botham lbw b Sarfraz	4
P. H. Edmonds not out	1
B 1, l-b 5, w 1, n-b 10	17
	(7 wkts) 119

1/0 2/24 3/51 4/77
5/102 6/110 7/116

C. M. Old and R. G. D. Willis did not bat.

Bowling: Sarfraz 20–6–39–5; Sikander 15–3–26–1; Mudassar 5–2–12–0; Qasim 11–8–11–0; Miandad 3–0–14–1.

Umpires: H. D. Bird and K. E. Palmer.

Match drawn.

ENGLAND v. NEW ZEALAND
FIRST CORNHILL TEST
At The Oval, July 27, 28, 29, 31, August 1, 1978

NEW ZEALAND

Batsman	First Innings		Second Innings	
J. G. Wright	c Radley b Willis	62	lbw b Botham	25
R. W. Anderson	b Old	4	c Taylor b Botham	2
G. P. Howarth	c Edmonds b Botham	94	b Willis	0
B. A. Edgar	c and b Miller	0	b Edmonds	38
*M. G. Burgess	lbw b Willis	38	lbw b Botham	7
B. E. Congdon	run out	7	b Botham	36
†G. N. Edwards	b Miller	2	c Brearley b Edmonds	11
R. J. Hadlee	c Brearley b Willis	6	b Edmonds	7
B. L. Cairns	lbw b Willis	5	b Miller	27
B. P. Bracewell	c Taylor b Willis	5	b Miller	0
S. L. Boock	not out	0	not out	0
	B 1, l-b 7, n-b 11	19	B 8, l-b 10, n-b 11	29
		234		**182**

1/7 2/130 3/131 4/191
5/197 6/207 7/224 8/230 9/230

1/15 2/19 3/30 4/70
5/86 6/105 7/113 8/182 9/182

Bowling: *First Innings*—Willis 20.2-9-42-5; Old 20-7-43-1; Botham 22-7-58-1; Miller 25-10-31-2; Edmonds 17-2-41-0. *Second Innings*—Willis 13-2-39-1; Old 5-2-13-0; Botham 19-2-46-3; Miller 34-19-35-2; Edmonds 34.1-23-20-4.

ENGLAND

Batsman	First Innings		Second Innings	
*J. M. Brearley	c Edwards b Bracewell	2	lbw b Boock	11
G. A. Gooch	lbw b Bracewell	0	not out	91
C. T. Radley	run out	49	lbw b Bracewell	2
D. I. Gower	run out	111	c Howarth b Cairns	11
G. R. J. Roope	b Boock	14	not out	10
G. Miller	lbw b Cairns	0		
I. T. Botham	c Bracewell b Boock	22		
†R. W. Taylor	c Edwards b Hadlee	8		
P. H. Edmonds	lbw b Hadlee	28		
C. M. Old	c Edwards b Cairns	16		
R. G. D. Willis	not out	3		
	B 15, l-b 8, n-b 3	26	B 2, l-b 3, n-b 8	13
		279	(3 wkts)	**138**

1/2 2/7 3/123 4/165
5/166 6/208 7/212 8/232 9/257

1/26 2/51 3/82

Bowling: *First Innings*—Hadlee 21.5-6-43-2; Bracewell 17-8-46-2; Cairns 40-16-65-2; Boock 35-18-61-2; Congdon 21-6-38-0. *Second Innings*—Hadlee 11.3-3-18-0; Bracewell 13-3-26-1; Cairns 7-0-21-1; Boock 20-5-55-1; Congdon 1-0-5-0:

Umpires: D. J. Constant and B. J. Meyer.

England won by seven wickets.

ENGLAND v. NEW ZEALAND
SECOND CORNHILL TEST
At Nottingham, August 10, 11, 12, 14, 1978

ENGLAND

Batsman	First Innings	
G. Boycott	c and b Hadlee	131
G. A. Gooch	c Burgess b Bracewell	55
C. T. Radley	lbw b Hadlee	59
D. I. Gower	c Cairns b Boock	46
*J. M. Brearley	c Parker b Bracewell	50
P. H. Edmonds	b Cairns	6
G. Miller	c Howarth b Hadlee	4
I. T. Botham	c Hadlee b Boock	8
†R. W. Taylor	b Hadlee	22
R. G. D. Willis	not out	1
M. Hendrick	c Edwards b Bracewell	7
	B 16, l-b 12, w 1, n-b 11	40
		429

1/111 2/240 3/301 4/342
5/350 6/364 7/374 8/419 9/427

Bowling: Hadlee 42-11-94-4; Bracewell 33.5-2-110-3; Cairns 38-7-85-1; Congdon 39-15-71-0; Boock 28-18-29-2.

NEW ZEALAND

Batsman	First Innings		Second Innings	
B. A. Edgar	c Taylor b Botham	6	c Botham b Edmonds	60
R. W. Anderson	lbw b Botham	19	run out	0
G. P. Howarth	not out	31	c Botham b Hendrick	34
S. L. Boock	c Taylor b Willis	8	b Edmonds	2
J. M. Parker	c Taylor b Hendrick	0	run out	38
*M. G. Burgess	c Taylor b Botham	5	c Brearley b Edmonds	7
B. E. Congdon	c Hendrick b Botham	27	c Brearley b Botham	4
†G. N. Edwards	c Taylor b Botham	0	c and b Edmonds	18
B. L. Cairns	b Edmonds	9	lbw b Botham	0
R. J. Hadlee	c Gooch b Botham	4	c Taylor b Botham	11
B. P. Bracewell	b Edmonds	0	not out	0
	L-b 1, w 1, n-b 9	11	L-b 6, w 1, n-b 9	16
		120		**190**

1/22 2/27 3/35 4/47 5/49
6/99 7/99 8/110 9/115

1/5 2/63 3/127 4/148
5/152 6/164 7/168 8/180 9/190

Bowling: *First Innings*—Willis 12-5-22-1; Hendrick 15-9-18-1; Botham 21-9-34-6; Edmonds 15.4-5-21-2; Miller 6-1-14-0. *Second Innings*—Willis 9-0-31-0; Hendrick 20-7-30-1; Botham 24-7-59-3; Edmonds 33.1-15-44-4; Miller 6-3-10-0.

Umpires: D. J. Constant and T. W. Spencer.

England won by an innings and 119 runs.

ENGLAND v. NEW ZEALAND
THIRD CORNHILL TEST
At Lord's, August 24, 25, 26, 28, 1978

NEW ZEALAND

J. G. Wright c Edmonds b Botham	17	b Botham	12
†B. A. Edgar c Edmonds b Emburey	39	b Botham	4
G. P. Howarth c Taylor b Botham	123	not out	14
J. M. Parker lbw b Hendrick	14	c Taylor b Botham	3
*M. G. Burgess lbw b Botham	68	c Hendrick b Botham	14
B. E. Congdon c Emburey b Botham	2	c Taylor b Willis	3
R. W. Anderson b Botham	16	c Taylor b Willis	1
R. J. Hadlee c Brearley b Botham	0	run out	5
R. O. Collinge c Emburey b Willis	19	b Botham	0
S. L. Boock not out	4	c Radley b Willis	0
B. P. Bracewell st Taylor b Emburey	4	c Hendrick b Willis	6
	33	L-b 3, n-b 8	11
B 4, l-b 18, 24, n-b 7			
	339		67

1/65 2/70 3/117 4/247 5/253
6/290 7/298 8/321 9/333

1/10 2/14 3/20 4/29
5/33 6/37 7/37 8/43 9/57

Bowling: *First Innings*—Willis 29–9–79–1; Hendrick 28–14–39–1; Botham 38–13–101–6; Edmonds 12–3–19–0; Emburey 26.1–12–39–2; Gooch 10–0–29–0. *Second Innings*—Willis 16–8–16–4; Botham 18.1–4–39–5; Emburey 3–2–1–0.

ENGLAND

G. A. Gooch c Boock b Hadlee	2	not out	42
G. Boycott c Hadlee b Bracewell	24	b Hadlee	4
C. T. Radley c Congdon b Hadlee	77	b Hadlee	0
D. I. Gower c Wright b Boock	71	c Congdon b Bracewell	46
*J. M. Brearley c Edgar b Hadlee	33	not out	8
I. T. Botham c Edgar b Collinge	21		
†R. W. Taylor lbw b Hadlee	1		
P. H. Edmonds c Edgar b Hadlee	5		
J. E. Emburey b Collinge	2		
M. Hendrick b Bracewell	12		
R. G. D. Willis not out	7		
B 7, l-b 5, n-b 22	34	L-b 3, w 4, n-b 11	18
	289	(3 wkts)	118

1/2 2/66 3/180 4/211 5/249
6/255 7/258 8/263 9/274

1/14 2/14 3/84

Bowling: *First Innings*—Hadlee 32–9–84–5; Collinge 30–9–58–2; Bracewell 19.3–1–58–2; Boock 25–10–33–1; Congdon 6–1–12–0. *Second Innings*—Hadlee 13.5–2–31–2; Collinge 6–1–26–0; Boock 5–1–11–0; Bracewell 6–0–32–1.

Umpires: H. D. Bird and B. J. Meyer.

England won by seven wickets.

AUSTRALIA v. ENGLAND
FIRST TEST MATCH
At Brisbane, December 1, 2, 3, 5, 6, 1978

AUSTRALIA

G. M. Wood c Taylor b Old	7	lbw b Old	19
G. J. Cosier run out	1	b Willis	0
P. M. Toohey b Willis	1	lbw b Botham	1
*G. N. Yallop c Gooch b Willis	7	c and b Willis	102
K. J. Hughes c Taylor b Botham	4	c Edmonds b Willis	129
T. J. Laughlin c sub (J. K. Lever) b Willis	2	lbw b Old	5
†J. A. Maclean not out	33	lbw b Miller	15
B. Yardley c Taylor b Willis	17	c Brearley b Miller	16
R. M. Hogg c Taylor b Botham	36	b Botham	16
A. G. Hurst c Taylor b Botham	0	b Botham	0
J. D. Higgs b Old	1	not out	0
L-b 1, n-b 6	7	B 9, l-b 5, n-b 22	36
	116		339

1/2 2/5 3/14 4/22 5/24
6/26 7/53 8/113 9/113

1/0 2/23 3/49 4/219
5/228 6/261 7/310 8/339 9/339

Bowling: *First Innings*—Willis 14–2–44–4; Old 9.7–1–24–2; Botham 12–1–40–3; Gooch 1–0–1–0; Edmonds 1–1–0–0. *Second Innings*—Willis 27.6–3–69–3; Old 17–1–60–2; Botham 26–5–95–3; Edmonds 12–1–27–C; Miller 34–12–52–2.

ENGLAND

G. Boycott c Hughes b Hogg	13	run out	16
G. A. Gooch c Laughlin b Hogg	2	c Yardley b Hogg	2
D. W. Randall c Laughlin b Hurst	75	not out	74
*R. W. Taylor lbw b Hurst	20		
*J. M. Brearley c Maclean b Hogg	6	c Maclean b Yardley	13
D. I. Gower c Maclean b Hurst	44	not out	48
I. T. Botham c Maclean b Hogg	49		
G. Miller lbw b Hogg	27		
P. H. Edmonds c Maclean b Hogg	1		
C. M. Old not out	29		
R. G. D. Willis c Maclean b Hurst	8		
B 7, l-b 4, n-b 1	12	B 12, l-b 3, n-b 2	17
	286	(3 wkts)	170

1/2 2/38 3/111 4/120 5/120
6/215 7/219 8/226 9/266

1/16 2/37 3/74

Bowling: *First Innings*—Hurst 27.4–6–93–4; Hogg 28–8–74–6; Laughlin 22–6–54–0; Yardley 7–1–34–0; Cosier 5–1–10–0; Higgs 6–2–9–0. *Second Innings*—Hurst 10–4–17–0; Hogg 12.5–2–35–1; Laughlin 3–0–6–0; Yardley 13–1–41–1; Cosier 3–0–11–0; Higgs 12–1–43–0.

Umpires: R. A. French and M. G. O'Connell.

England won by seven wickets.

AUSTRALIA v. ENGLAND
SECOND TEST MATCH
At Perth, December 15, 16, 17, 19, 20, 1978

ENGLAND

Batsman	1st Innings		2nd Innings	
G. Boycott	lbw b Hurst	77	lbw b Hogg	23
G. A. Gooch	c Maclean b Hogg	1	lbw b Hogg	43
D. W. Randall	c Wood b Hogg	0	c Cosier b Yardley	45
*J. M. Brearley	c Maclean b Dymock	17	c Maclean b Hogg	0
D. I. Gower	b Hogg	102	c Maclean b Hogg	12
I. T. Botham	lbw b Hurst	11	c Wood b Yardley	30
G. Miller	b Hogg	40	c Toohey b Yardley	25
†R. W. Taylor	c Hurst b Yardley	12	c Maclean b Hogg	2
J. K. Lever	c Cosier b Hurst	14	c Maclean b Hurst	10
R. G. D. Willis	c Yallop b Hogg	2	not out	3
M. Hendrick	not out	7	b Dymock	1
Extras	B 6, l-b 9, w 3, n-b 8	26	L-b 6, n-b 8	14
Total		**309**		**208**

1/3 2/3 3/41 4/199 5/219 6/224 7/253 8/295 9/300

1/58 2/93 3/93 4/135 5/151 6/176 7/201 8/201 9/206

Bowling: *First Innings*—Hogg 30.5-9-65-5; Dymock 34-4-72-1; Hurst 26-7-70-3; Yardley 23-1-62-1; Cosier 4-2-14-0. *Second Innings*—Hogg 17-5-43-1; Dymock 16.3-2-53-1; Hurst 17-5-43-1; Yardley 16-1-41-3.

AUSTRALIA

Batsman	1st Innings		2nd Innings	
G. M. Wood	lbw b Lever	5	c Taylor b Lever	64
W. M. Darling	run out	25	c Boycott b Lever	5
K. J. Hughes	b Willis	16	c Gooch b Willis	12
*G. N. Yallop	b Willis	3	c Taylor b Hendrick	3
P. M. Toohey	not out	81	c Taylor b Hendrick	0
G. J. Cosier	c Gooch b Willis	4	lbw b Miller	47
†J. A. Maclean	c Gooch b Miller	0	c Brearley b Miller	1
B. Yardley	c Taylor b Hendrick	12	c Botham b Lever	7
R. M. Hogg	c Taylor b Willis	18	b Miller	0
G. Dymock	b Hendrick	11	not out	6
A. G. Hurst	c Taylor b Willis	5	b Lever	5
Extras	L-b 7, w 1, n-b 2	10	L-b 3, w 4, n-b 4	11
Total		**190**		**161**

1/8 2/34 3/38 4/60 5/78 6/79 7/100 8/128 9/185

1/8 2/36 3/58 4/58 5/141 6/143 7/143 8/147 9/151

Bowling: *First Innings*—Lever 7-0-20-1; Botham 11-2-46-0; Willis 18.5-5-44-5; Hendrick 14-1-39-2; Miller 16-6-31-1. *Second Innings*—Lever 8.1-2-28-4; Botham 11-1-54-0; Willis 12-1-36-1; Hendrick 8-3-11-2; Miller 7-4-21-3.

Umpires: R. C. Bailhache and T. F. Brooks.

England won by 166 runs.

AUSTRALIA v. ENGLAND
THIRD TEST MATCH
At Melbourne, December 29, 30, 1978, January 1, 2, 3, 1979

AUSTRALIA

Batsman	1st Innings		2nd Innings	
G. M. Wood	c Emburey b Miller	100	b Botham	34
W. M. Darling	run out	33	c Randall b Miller	21
K. J. Hughes	c Taylor b Botham	0	c Gower b Botham	48
*G. N. Yallop	c Hendrick b Botham	41	c Taylor b Miller	16
P. M. Toohey	c Randall b Miller	32	c Botham b Emburey	20
A. R. Border	c Brearley b Hendrick	29	run out	0
†J. A. Maclean	b Botham	8	c Hendrick b Emburey	10
R. M. Hogg	c Randall b Miller	0	b Botham	1
G. Dymock	b Hendrick	0	c Brearley b Hendrick	6
A. G. Hurst	b Hendrick	0	not out	0
J. D. Higgs	not out	0	st Taylor b Emburey	0
Extras	L-b 8, n-b 6	14	B 4, l-b 6, n-b 1	11
Total		**258**		**167**

1/65 2/65 3/126 4/189 5/247 6/250 7/250 8/251 9/252

1/55 2/81 3/101 4/136 5/136 6/152 7/157 8/167 9/167

Bowling: *First Innings*—Willis 13-2-47-0; Botham 20.1-4-68-3; Hendrick 23-3-50-3; Emburey 14-1-44-0; Miller 19-6-35-3. *Second Innings*—Willis 7-0-21-0; Botham 15-4-41-3; Hendrick 14-4-25-1; Emburey 21.2-12-30-3; Miller 14-5-39-2.

ENGLAND

Batsman	1st Innings		2nd Innings	
G. Boycott	b Hogg	1	lbw b Hurst	38
*J. M. Brearley	lbw b Hogg	1	c Maclean b Dymock	0
D. W. Randall	lbw b Hurst	13	lbw b Hogg	2
G. A. Gooch	c Border b Dymock	25	lbw b Hogg	40
D. I. Gower	lbw b Dymock	29	b Hogg	49
I. T. Botham	c Darling b Higgs	22	c Maclean b Higgs	10
G. Miller	b Hogg	7	c Hughes b Higgs	1
†R. W. Taylor	b Hogg	1	c Maclean b Hogg	5
J. E. Emburey	b Hogg	0	not out	7
R. G. D. Willis	c Darling b Dymock	19	c Yallop b Hogg	0
M. Hendrick	not out	6	b Hogg	3
Extras	B 6, l-b 4, n-b 9	19	B 10, l-b 7, w 1, n-b 6	24
Total		**143**		**179**

1/2 2/3 3/40 4/52 5/81 6/100 7/101 8/101 9/120

1/1 2/6 3/71 4/122 5/163 6/163 7/167 8/171 9/179

Bowling: *First Innings*—Hogg 17-7-30-5; Hurst 12-2-24-1; Dymock 15.6-4-38-3; Higgs 9-9-32-1. *Second Innings*—Hogg 17-5-36-5; Hurst 11-1-39-1; Dymock 18-4-37-2; Higgs 16-2-29-2; Border 5-0-14-0.

Umpires: R. A. French and M. G. O'Connell.

Australia won by 103 runs.

AUSTRALIA v. ENGLAND
FOURTH TEST MATCH
At Sydney, January 6, 7, 8, 10, 11, 1979

ENGLAND

Batsman	1st Innings		2nd Innings	
G. Boycott	c Border b Hurst	8	lbw b Hogg	0
*J. M. Brearley	b Hogg	17	b Border	53
D. W. Randall	c Wood b Hurst	0	lbw b Hogg	150
G. A. Gooch	c Toohey b Higgs	18	c Wood b Higgs	22
D. I. Gower	c Maclean b Hurst	7	c Maclean b Hogg	34
I. T. Botham	c Yallop b Hogg	59	c Wood b Higgs	6
G. Miller	c Maclean b Hurst	4	lbw b Hogg	17
†R. W. Taylor	c Border b Higgs	10	run out	21
J. E. Emburey	c Wood by Higgs	0	c Darling b Higgs	14
R. G. D. Willis	not out	7	c Darling b Hogg	0
M. Hendrick	b Hurst	10	c Toohey b Higgs	7
Extras	B 1, l-b 1, w 2, n-b 8	12	B 5, l-b 3, n-b 14	22
Total		**152**		**346**

1/18 2/18 3/35 4/51 5/66 6/70 7/94 8/98 9/141

1/0 2/111 3/169 4/237 5/267 6/292 7/307 8/334 9/334

Bowling: *First Innings*—Hogg 11–3–36–2; Dymock 13–1–34–0; Hurst 10.6–2–28–5; Higgs 18–4–42–3. *Second Innings*—Hogg 28–10–67–4; Dymock 17–4–35–0; Hurst 19–3–43–0; Higgs 59.6–15–148–5; Border 23–11–31–1.

AUSTRALIA

Batsman	1st Innings		2nd Innings	
G. M. Wood	b Willis	0	run out	27
W. M. Darling	c Botham b Miller	91	c Gooch b Hendrick	13
K. J. Hughes	c Emburey b Willis	48	c Emburey b Miller	15
*G. N. Yallop	b Hendrick	44	c and b Hendrick	1
P. M. Toohey	c Gooch b Botham	1	b Miller	5
A. R. Border	not out	60	not out	45
†J. A. Maclean	lbw b Emburey	12	c Botham b Miller	0
R. M. Hogg	run out	6	c Botham b Emburey	0
G. Dymock	b Botham	5	b Emburey	0
J. D. Higgs	c Botham b Hendrick	11	lbw b Emburey	3
A. G. Hurst	run out	0	b Emburey	0
Extras	B 2, l-b 3, n-b 11	16	L-b 1, n-b 1	2
Total		**294**		**111**

1/1 2/126 3/178 4/179 5/210 6/235 7/245 8/276 9/290

1/38 2/44 3/45 4/59 5/74 6/76 7/85 8/85 9/105

Bowling: *First Innings*—Willis 9–2–33–2; Botham 28–3–87–2; Hendrick 24–4–50–2; Miller 13–2–37–1; Emburey 29–10–57–1; Gooch 5–1–14–0. *Second Innings*—Willis 2–0–8–0; Hendrick 10–3–17–2; Miller 20–7–38–3; Emburey 17.2–2–46–4.

Umpires: R. C. Bailhache and R. A. French.

England won by 93 runs.

AUSTRALIA v. ENGLAND
FIFTH TEST MATCH
At Adelaide, January 27, 28, 29, 31, February 1, 1979

ENGLAND

Batsman	1st Innings		2nd Innings	
G. Boycott	c Wright b Hurst	6	c Hughes b Hurst	49
*J. M. Brearley	c Wright b Hurst	2	lbw b Carlson	9
D. W. Randall	c Carlson b Hurst	4	c Yardley b Hurst	15
G. A. Gooch	c Hughes b Hogg	1	b Carlson	18
D. I. Gower	lbw b Hurst	9	lbw b Higgs	21
I. T. Botham	c Wright b Higgs	74	c Yardley b Hurst	7
G. Miller	lbw b Hogg	31	c Wright b Hurst	64
†R. W. Taylor	run out	4	c Wright b Hogg	97
J. E. Emburey	b Higgs	4	b Hogg	42
R. G. D. Willis	c Darling b Hogg	24	c Wright b Hogg	12
M. Hendrick	not out	0	not out	3
Extras	B 1, l-b 4, w 3, n-b 2	10	B 1, l-b 16, w 2, n-b 4	23
Total		**169**		**360**

1/10 2/12 3/16 4/18 5/27 6/80 7/113 8/136 9/147

1/31 2/57 3/97 4/106 5/130 6/132 7/267 8/336 9/347

Bowling: *First Innings*—Hogg 10.4–1–26–4; Hurst 14–1–65–3; Carlson 9–1–34–0; Yardley 4–0–25–0; Higgs 3–1–9–2. *Second Innings*—Hogg 27.6–7–59–3; Hurst 37–9–97–4; Carlson 27–8–41–2; Yardley 20–6–60–0; Higgs 28–4–75–1; Border 3–2–5–0.

AUSTRALIA

Batsman	1st Innings		2nd Innings	
W. M. Darling	c Willis b Botham	15	c Willis b Botham	18
G. M. Wood	c Randall b Emburey	35	run out	9
K. J. Hughes	c Emburey b Hendrick	4	c Gower b Hendrick	46
*G. N. Yallop	b Hendrick	0	b Hendrick	36
A. R. Border	c Taylor b Botham	11	b Willis	1
P. H. Carlson	c Taylor b Botham	0	c Gower b Hendrick	21
B. Yardley	b Botham	28	c Brearley b Willis	0
†K. J. Wright	lbw b Emburey	29	c Emburey b Miller	0
R. M. Hogg	b Willis	0	b Miller	2
J. D. Higgs	run out	16	not out	3
A. G. Hurst	not out	17	b Willis	13
Extras	B 1, l-b 3, n-b 5	9	L-b 1, n-b 10	11
Total		**164**		**160**

1/5 2/10 3/22 4/24 5/72 6/94 7/114 8/116 9/133

1/31 2/36 3/115 4/120 5/121 6/121 7/124 8/130 9/147

Bowling: *First Innings*—Willis 11–1–55–1; Hendrick 19–1–45–2; Botham 11.4–0–42–4; Emburey 12–7–13–2. *Second Innings*—Willis 12–3–41–3; Hendrick 14–6–19–3; Botham 14–4–37–1; Emburey 9–5–16–0; Miller 18–3–36–2.

Umpires: R. C. Bailhache and M. G. O'Connell.

England won by 205 runs.

AUSTRALIA v. ENGLAND
SIXTH TEST MATCH
At Sydney, February 10, 11, 12, 14, 1979

AUSTRALIA

G. M. Wood c Botham b Hendrick	15	c Willis b Miller	29
A. M. J. Hilditch run out	3	c Taylor b Hendrick	1
K. J. Hughes c Botham b Willis	16	c Gooch b Emburey	7
*G. N. Yallop c Gower b Botham	121	c Taylor b Miller	17
P. M. Toohey c Taylor b Botham	8	c Gooch b Emburey	0
P. H. Carlson c Gooch b Botham	2	c Botham b Emburey	0
B. Yardley b Emburey	7	not out	61
†K. J. Wright st Taylor b Emburey	3	c Boycott b Miller	5
R. M. Hogg c Emburey b Miller	9	b Miller	7
J. D. Higgs not out	9	c Botham b Emburey	2
A. G. Hurst b Botham	0	c and b Miller	4
L-b 3, n-b 2	5	B 3, l-b 6, n-b 1	10
	198		143

1/18 2/19 3/67 4/101 5/109
6/116 7/124 8/159 9/198

1/1 8 2/28 3/48 4/48
5/48 6/82 7/114 8/130 9/136

Bowling: *First Innings*—Willis 11–4–48–1; Hendrick 12–2–21–1; Botham 9.7–1–57–4; Emburey 18–3–48–2; Miller 9–3–13–1; Boycott 1–0–6–0. *Second Innings*—Willis 3–0–15–0; Hendrick 7–3–22–1; Emburey 24–4–52–4; Miller 27.1–6–44–5.

ENGLAND

G. Boycott c Hilditch b Hurst	19	c Hughes b Higgs	13
*J. M. Brearley c Toohey b Higgs	46	not out	20
D. W. Randall lbw b Hogg	7	not out	0
G. A. Gooch st Wright b Higgs	74		
D. I. Gower c Wright b Higgs	65		
I. T. Botham c Carlson b Yardley	23		
G. Miller lbw b Hurst	18		
†R. W. Taylor not out	36		
J. E. Emburey c Hilditch b Hurst	0		
R. G. D. Willis b Higgs	10		
M. Hendrick c and b Yardley	10	N-b 2	2
B 3, l-b 5, n-b 2	10		
	308	(1 wkt)	35

1/37 2/46 3/115 4/182 5/233
6/247 7/270 8/280 9/306

1/31

Bowling: *First Innings*—Hogg 18–6–42–1; Hurst 20–4–58–3; Yardley 25–2–105–2; Carlson 10–1–24–0; Higgs 30–8–69–4. *Second Innings*—Yardley 5.2–0–21–0; Higgs 5–1–12–1.

Umpires: A. R. Crafter and D. G. Weser.

England won by nine wickets.

ENGLAND v. INDIA
FIRST CORNHILL TEST
At Birmingham, July 12, 13, 14, 16, 1979

ENGLAND

*J. M. Brearley c Reddy b Dev	24
G. Boycott lbw b Dev	155
D. W. Randall c Reddy b Dev	15
G. A. Gooch c Reddy b Dev	83
D. I. Gower not out	200
I. T. Botham b Dev	33
G. Miller not out	63
B 4, l-b 27, w 11, n-b 18	60
(5 wkts dec)	633

1/66 2/90 3/235 4/426 5/468

P. H. Edmonds, †R. W. Taylor, R. G. D. Willis and M. Hendrick did not bat.

Bowling: Kapil Dev 48–15–146–5; Ghavri 38–5 129–0; Amarnath 13.2–2–47–0; Chandrasekhar 29–1–113–0; Venkataraghavan 31–4–107– ; Gaekwad 3–0–12–0; Chauhan 3–0–19–0.

INDIA

S. M. Gavaskar run out	61	c Gooch b Hendrick	68
C. P. S. Chauhan c Gooch b Botham	4	c Randall b Willis	56
D. B. Vengsarkar c Gooch b Edmonds	22	c Edmonds b Hendrick	7
G. R. Viswanath c Botham b Edmonds	78	c Taylor b Botham	51
A. D. Gaekwad c Botham b Willis	25	c Gooch b Botham	15
M. Amarnath b Willis	31	lbw b Botham	10
Kapil Dev lbw b Botham	1	c Hendrick b Botham	21
K. D. Ghavri c Brearley b Willis	6	c Randall b Hendrick	4
†B. Reddy b Hendrick	21	lbw b Hendrick	0
*S. Venkataraghavan c Botham b Hendrick	28	lbw b Botham	0
B. S. Chandrasekhar not out	0	not out	21
B 1, l-b 4, w 3, n-b 12	20	B 7, l-b 12, n-b 2	21
	297		253

1/15 2/59 3/129 4/205
5/209 6/210 7/229 8/251 9/294

1/124 2/136 3/136 4/182
5/227 6/240 7/249 8/250 9/251

Bowling: *First Innings*—Willis 24–9–69–3; Botham 26–4–86–2; Hendrick 24.1–9–36–2; Edmonds 26–11–60–2; Boycott 5–1–8–0; Miller 11–3–18–0. *Second Innings*—Willis 14–3–45–1; Botham 29–8–70–5; Hendrick 20.4–8–45–4; Edmonds 17–6–37–0; Miller 9–1–27–0; Gooch 6–3–8–0.

Umpires: D. J. Constant and B. J. Meyer.

England won by an innings and 83 runs.

ENGLAND v. INDIA
SECOND CORNHILL TEST
At Lord's, August 2, 3, 4, 6, 7, 1979

INDIA

S. M. Gavaskar c Taylor b Gooch	42	c Brearley b Botham	59
C. P. S. Chauhan c Randall b Botham	2	c Randall b Edmonds	31
D. B. Vengsarkar c Botham b Brearley	0	c Boycott b Edmonds	103
G. R. Viswanath c Brearley b Hendrick	21	c Gower b Lever	113
A. D. Gaekwad c Taylor b Botham	13	not out	1
Yashpal Sharma c Taylor b Botham	11	not out	5
Kapil Dev c Miller b Botham	4		
K. D. Ghavri not out	3		
*B. Reddy lbw b Botham	0		
*S. Venkataraghavan run out	0		
B. S. Bedi b Lever	0		
		B 2, l-b 2, w 1, n-b 1	6

1/12 2/23 3/51 4/75   96   1/79 2/99 3/309 4/312   (4 wkts) 318
5/79 6/89 7/96 8/96 9/96

Bowling: First Innings—Lever 9.5–3–29–1; Botham 19–9–35–5; Hendrick 15–7–15–2; Edmonds 2–1–1–0; Gooch 10–5–16–1. Second Innings—Lever 24–7–69–1; Botham 35–13–80–1; Hendrick 25–12–56–0; Edmonds 45–18–62–2; Gooch 2–0–8–0; Miller 17–6–37–0.

ENGLAND

*J. M. Brearley c Reddy b Dev	12
G. Boycott c Gavaskar b Ghavri	32
G. A. Gooch b Dev	10
D. I. Gower b Ghavri	82
D. W. Randall run out	57
I. T. Botham b Venkataraghavan	36
G. Miller st Reddy b Bedi	62
P. H. Edmonds c Reddy b Dev	20
†R. W. Taylor c Vengsarkar b Bedi	64
J. K. Lever not out	6
B 11, l-b 21, w 2, n-b 4	38

(9 wkts dec) 419
M. Hendrick did not bat.

1/21 2/60 3/71 4/185
5/226 6/253 7/291 8/394 9/419

Bowling: Kapil Dev 38–11–93–3; Ghavri 31–2–122–2; Bedi 35.5–13–87–2; Venkataraghavan 22–2–79–1.

Umpires: H. D. Bird and K. E. Palmer.

Match drawn.

ENGLAND v. INDIA
THIRD CORNHILL TEST
At Leeds, August 16, 17, 18, 20, 21, 1979

ENGLAND

G. Boycott c Viswanath b Dev	31
*J. M. Brearley c Viswanath b Amarnath	15
G. A. Gooch c Vengsarkar b Dev	4
D. I. Gower lbw b Dev	0
D. W. Randall b Ghavri	11
I. T. Botham c Ghavri b Venkat	137
G. Miller c Reddy b Amarnath	27
P. H. Edmonds run out	18
†R. W. Taylor c Chauhan b Bedi	1
R. G. D. Willis not out	4
M. Hendrick c sub (Singh) b Bedi	0
B 4, l-b 6, w 4, n-b 8	22

270

1/53 2/57 3/57 4/58
5/89 6/176 7/264 8/264 9/266

Bowling: Kapil Dev 27–7–84–3; Ghavri 18–4–60–1; Amarnath 20–7–53–2; Venkataraghavan 7–2–25–1; Bedi 8.5–2–26–2.

INDIA

S. M. Gavaskar b Edmonds	78
C. P. S. Chauhan c Botham b Willis	0
M. Amarrath c Taylor b Willis	0
G. R. Viswanath c Brearley b Hendrick	1
Yashpal Sharma c Botham b Miller	40
D. B. Vengsarkar not out	65
Kapil Dev c Gooch b Miller	3
K. D. Ghavri not out	20
B 11, l-b 4, w 1	16

(6 wkts) 223

1/1 2/9 3/12 4/106 5/156 6/160

*S. Venkataraghavan, B. S. Bedi and †B. Reddy did not bat.

Bowling: Willis 18–5–42–2; Hendrick 14–6–13–1; Botham 13–3–39–0; Edmonds 28–8–59–1; Miller 32–13–52–2; Gooch 3–1–2–0; Boycott 2–2–0–0.

Umpires: H. D. Bird and B. J. Meyer.

Match drawn.

ENGLAND V. INDIA
FOURTH CORNHILL TEST
At The Oval, August 30, 31, September 1, 3, 4, 1979

ENGLAND

Batsman	1st innings		2nd innings	
G. Boycott	lbw b Dev	35	b Ghavri	125
A. R. Butcher	c Singh b Venkat	14	c Venkat b Ghavri	20
G. A. Gooch	c Viswanath b Ghavri	79	lbw b Dev	31
D. I. Gower	lbw b Dev	0	c Reddy b Bedi	7
P. Willey	c Singh b Bedi	52	c Reddy b Ghavri	31
I. T. Botham	st Reddy b Venkat	38	run out	0
*J. M. Brearley	b Ghavri	34	b Venkat	11
†D. L. Bairstow	c Reddy b Dev	9	c Gavaskar b Dev	59
P. H. Edmonds	c Dev b Venkat	16	not out	27
R. G. D. Willis	not out	10		
M. Hendrick	c Gavaskar b Bedi	0		
Extras	L-b 9, w 4, n-b 5	18	L-b 14, w 2, n-b 7	23
		305	(8 wkts dec)	**334**

1/45 2/51 3/51 4/148 5/203 6/245 7/272 8/275 9/304

1/43 2/107 3/125 4/192 5/194 6/215 7/291 8/334

Bowling: *First Innings*—Kapil Dev 32-12-83-3; Ghavri 26-8-61-2; Bedi 29.5-4-69-2; Singh 8-2-15-0; Venkataraghavan 29-9-59-3. *Second Innings*—Kapil Dev 28.5-4-89-2; Ghavri 34-11-76-3; Bedi 26-4-67-1; Singh 2-0-4-0; Ventkataraghavan 26-4-75-1.

INDIA

Batsman	1st innings		2nd innings	
S. M. Gavaskar	c Bairstow b Botham	13	c Gower b Botham	221
C. P. S. Chauhan	c Botham b Willis	6	c Botham b Willis	80
D. B. Vengsarkar	c Botham b Willis	0	c Botham b Edmonds	52
G. R. Viswanath	c Brearley b Botham	62	c Brearley b Willey	15
Yashpal Sharma	lbw b Willis	27	lbw b Botham	19
Yajurvindra Singh	not out	43	lbw b Botham	1
Kapil Dev	b Hendrick	16	c Gooch b Willey	0
†B. Reddy	c Bairstow b Botham	12	not out	3
*S. Venkataraghavan	c and b Hendrick	2	not out	5
B. S. Bedi	c Brearley b Hendrick	1	run out	6
Extras	B 2, l-b 3, w 5, n-b 3	13	B 11, l-b 15, w 1	27
		202	(8 wkts)	**429**

1/9 2/9 3/47 4/91 5/130 6/161 7/172 8/192 9/200

1/213 2/366 3/367 4/389 5/410 6/411 7/419 8/423

Bowling: *First Innings*—Willis 18-2-53-3; Botham 28-7-65-4; Hendrick 22.3-7-38-3; Willey 4-1-10-0; Gooch 2-0-6-0; Edmonds 5-1-17-0. *Second Innings*—Willis 28-4-89-1; Botham 29-5-97-3; Hendrick 8-2-15-0; Willey 43.5-14-96-2; Gooch 2-0-9-0; Edmonds 38-11-87-1; Butcher 2-0-9-0.

Match drawn.

Umpires: D. J. Constant and K. E. Palmer.

AUSTRALIA *v.* ENGLAND
FIRST TEST MATCH
At Perth, December 14, 15, 16, 18, 19, 1979

AUSTRALIA

Batsman	1st innings		2nd innings	
J. M. Wiener	run out	11	c Randall b Underwood	58
B. M. Laird	lbw b Botham	0	c Taylor b Underwood	33
A. R. Border	lbw b Botham	4	c Taylor b Willis	115
*G. S. Chappell	c Boycott b Botham	19	st Taylor b Underwood	43
K. J. Hughes	c Brearley b Underwood	99	c Miller b Botham	4
P. M. Toohey	c Underwood b Dilley	19	c Taylor b Botham	3
†R. W. Marsh	c Taylor b Dilley	42	c Gower b Botham	4
R. J. Bright	c Taylor b Botham	17	lbw b Botham	12
D. K. Lillee	c Taylor b Botham	18	c Willey b Dilley	19
G. Dymock	b Botham	5	not out	20
J. R. Thomson	not out	1	b Botham	8
Extras	B 4, l-b 3, n-b 2	9	B 4, l-b 5, w 2, n-b 7	18
		244		**337**

1/2 2/17 3/20 4/88 5/127 6/186 7/219 8/219 9/243

1/91 2/100 3/168 4/183 5/191 6/204 7/225 8/303 9/323

Bowling: *First Innings*—Dilley 18-1-47-2; Botham 35-9-78-6; Willis 23-7-47-0; Underwood 13-4-33-1; Miller 11-2-30-0. *Second Innings*—Botham 45.5-14-98-5; Dilley 18-3-50-1; Willis 26-7-52-1; Miller 10-0-36-0; Underwood 41-14-82-3; Willey 1-0-1-0.

ENGLAND

Batsman	1st innings		2nd innings	
D. W. Randall	c Hughes b Lillee	0	lbw b Dymock	1
G. Boycott	lbw b Lillee	0	not out	99
P. Willey	c Chappell b Dymock	9	lbw b Dymock	12
D. I. Gower	c Marsh b Lillee	17	c Thomson b Dymock	23
G. Miller	c Hughes b Thomson	25	c Chappell b Thomson	8
*J. M. Brearley	c Marsh b Lillee	64	c Marsh b Bright	11
I. T. Botham	c Toohey b Thomson	15	c Marsh b Lillee	18
†R. W. Taylor	b Chappell	14	b Lillee	15
G. R. Dilley	not out	38	c Marsh b Dymock	15
D. L. Underwood	lbw b Dymock	13	c Wiener b Dymock	16
R. G. D. Willis	b Dymock	11	c Chappell b Dymock	0
Extras	L-b 7, n-b 15	22	L-b 3, w 1, n-b 8	12
		228		**215**

1/0 2/12 3/144 4/15 5/74 6/90 7/123 8/185 9/203

1/8 2/26 3/64 4/75 5/115 6/141 7/182 8/211 9/211

Bowling: *First Innings*—Lillee 28-11-73-4; Dymock 29.1-14-52-3; Chappell 11-6-5-1; Thomson 21-3-70-2; Bright 1-0-6-0. *Second Innings*—Lillee 23-5-74-2; Dymock 17.2-4-34-6; Chappell 6-4-6-0; Thomson 11-3-30-1; Bright 23-11-30-1; Wiener 8-3-22-0; Border 2-0-7-0.

Australia won by 138 runs.

Umpires: M. O'Connell and D. Weser.

AUSTRALIA v. ENGLAND
SECOND TEST MATCH
At Sydney, January 4, 5, 6, 8, 1980

ENGLAND

G. A. Gooch b Lillee	18	c G. S. Chappell b Dymock 4
G. Boycott b Dymock	8	c McCosker b Pascoe 18
D. W. Randall c G. S. Chappell b Lillee	0	c Marsh b G. S. Chappell 25
P. Willey c Wiener b Dymock	8	b Pascoe 3
*J. M. Brearley c Pascoe b Dymock	7	c Marsh b Pascoe 19
D. I. Gower b G. S. Chappell	3	not out 98
I. T. Botham c G. S. Chappell b Pascoe	27	c Wiener b G. S. Chappell 0
†R. W. Taylor c Marsh by Lillee	10	b Lillee 8
G. R. Dilley not out	22	b Dymock 4
R. G. D. Willis c Wiener b Dymock	3	c G. S. Chappell b Lillee 1
D. L. Underwood c Border b Lillee	12	c Border by Dymock 43
N-b 5	5	B 1, l-b 10, w 1, n-b 2 14
	123	237

1/10 2/13 3/14 4/38 5/41 6/74 7/75 8/90 9/98
1/6 2/21 3/29 4/77 5/105 6/156 7/174 8/211 9/218

Bowling: *First Innings*—Lillee 13.3-4-40-4; Dymock 17-6-42-4; Pascoe 9-4-14-1; G. S. Chappell 4-1-19-1; Higgs 1-0-3-0. *Second Innings*—Lillee 24.3-3-63-2; Dymock 28-8-48-3; Pascoe 23-3-76-3; G. S. Chappell 21-10-36-2.

AUSTRALIA

R. B. McCosker c Gower b Willis	1	c Taylor b Underwood 41
J. M. Wiener run out	22	b Underwood 13
I. M. Chappell c Brearley b Gooch	42	c Botham b Underwood 9
*G. S. Chappell c Taylor b Underwood	3	not out 98
K. J. Hughes c Taylor b Botham	18	c Dilley b Willis 47
A. R. Border c Gooch b Botham	15	not out 2
†R. W. Marsh c Underwood b Gooch	7	
D. K. Lillee c Brearley b Botham	5	
G. Dymock c Taylor b Botham	4	
L. S. Pascoe not out	10	
J. D. Higgs b Underwood	2	
B 2, l-b 12, w 2	16	L-b 8, w 1 9
	145	(4 wkts) 219

1/18 2/52 3/71 4/92 5/100 6/114 7/121 8/129 9/132
1/31 2/51 3/98 4/203

Bowling: *First Innings*—Botham 17-7-29-4; Willis 11-3-30-1; Underwood 13.2-3-39-2; Dilley 5-1-13-0; Willey 1-0-2-0; Gooch 11-4-16-2. *Second Innings*—Botham 23.3-12-43-0; Willis 12-2-26-1; Underwood 26-6-71-3; Dilley 12-0-33-0; Willey 4-0-17-0; Gooch 8-2-20-0.

Umpires: R. C. Bailhache and W. J. Copeland.

Australia won by six wickets.

AUSTRALIA v. ENGLAND
THIRD TEST MATCH
At Melbourne, February 1, 2, 3, 5, 6, 1980

ENGLAND

G. A. Gooch run out	99	b Mallett 81
G. Boycott c Mallett b Dymock	44	b Lillee 7
W. Larkins c G. S. Chappell b Pascoe	25	lbw b Pascoe 3
D. I. Gower lbw b Lillee	0	b Lillee 11
P. Willey lbw b Pascoe	1	c Marsh b Lillee 2
I. T. Botham c Marsh b Lillee	8	not out 119
*J. M. Brearley not out	60	c Border b Pascoe 10
†R. W. Taylor b Lillee	23	c Border b Lillee 32
D. L. Underwood c I. M. Chappell b Lillee	3	b Pascoe 0
J. K. Lever b Lillee	22	c Marsh b Lillee 12
R. G. D. Willis c G. S. Chappell b Lillee	4	c G. S. Chappell b Pascoe 2
B 1, l-b 2, n-b 14	17	B 2, l-b 12, n-b 10 24
	306	273

1/116 2/170 3/175 4/177 5/177 6/192 7/238 8/242 9/296
1/25 2/46 3/64 4/67 5/88 6/92 7/178 8/179 9/268

Bowling: *First Innings*—Lillee 33.1-9-60-6; Dymock 28-6-54-1; Mallett 35-9-104-0; Pascoe 32-7-71-2. *Second Innings*—Lillee 33-6-78-5; Dymock 11-2-30-0; Mallett 14-1-45-1; Pascoe 29.5-3-80-4; Border 4-0-16-0.

AUSTRALIA

R. B. McCosker c Botham b Underwood	33	lbw b Botham 2
B. M. Laird c Gower b Underwood	74	c Boycott b Underwood 25
I. M. Chappell c and b Underwood	75	not out 20
K. J. Hughes c Underwood b Botham	15	
A. R. Border c and b Lever	63	
*G. S. Chappell c Larkins b Lever	114	not out 40
†R. W. Marsh c Botham b Lever	17	
D. K. Lillee c Willey b Lever	8	
G. Dymock b Botham	19	
A. A. Mallett lbw b Botham	25	
L. S. Pascoe not out	1	
B 13, l-b 12, n-b 7, w 1	33	L-b 8, n-b 2 10
	477	(2 wkts) 103

1/52 2/179 3/196 4/219 5/345 6/411 7/421 8/432 9/465
1/20 2/42

Bowling: *First Innings*—Lever 53-15-111-4; Botham 39.5-15-105-3; Willis 21-4-61-0; Underwood 53-19-131-3; Willey 13-2-36-0. *Second Innings*—Lever 7.4-3-18-0; Botham 12-5-18-1; Willis 5-3-8-0; Underwood 14-2-49-1.

Umpires: R. C. Bailhache and P. M. Cronin.

Australia won by eight wickets.

INDIA v. ENGLAND
JUBILEE TEST MATCH
At Bombay, February 15, 17, 18, 19, 1980

INDIA

S. M. Gavaskar c Taylor b Botham	49	c Taylor b Botham 24
R. M. Binny run out	15	lbw b Botham 0
D. B. Vengsarkar c Taylor b Stevenson	34	lbw b Lever 10
*G. R. Viswanath b Lever	11	c Taylor b Botham 5
S. M. Patil c Taylor b Botham	30	lbw b Botham 0
Yashpal Sharma lbw b Botham	21	lbw b Botham 27
Kapil Dev c Taylor b Botham	0	not out 45
†S. M. H. Kirmani not out	40	c Gooch b Botham 0
K. D. Ghavri c Taylor b Stevenson	11	c Brearley b Lever 5
Shivlal Yadav c Taylor b Botham	8	c Taylor b Botham 15
D. R. Doshi c Taylor b Botham	6	c and b Lever 0
B 5, l-b 3, n-b 9	17	B 4, l-b 8, w 1, n-b 5 18
	242	**149**

1/56 2/102 3/108 4/135 5/160
6/160 7/181 8/197 9/223

1/4 2/22 3/31 4/31 5/56
6/58 7/102 8/115 9/148

Bowling: *First Innings*—Lever 23–3–82–1; Botham 22.5–7–58–6; Stevenson 14–1–59–2; Underwood 6–1–23–0; Gooch 4–2–3–0. *Second Innings*—Lever 20.2–2–65–3; Botham 26–7–48–7; Stevenson 5–1–13–0; Underwood 1–0–5–0.

ENGLAND

G. A. Gooch c Kirmani b Ghavri	8	not out 49
G. Boycott c Kirmani b Binny	22	not out 43
W. Larkins lbw b Ghavri	0	
D. I. Gower lbw b Dev	16	
*J. M. Brearley lbw b Dev	5	
I. T. Botham lbw b Ghavri	114	
†R. W. Taylor lbw b Dev	43	
J. E. Emburey c Binny b Ghavri	8	
J. K. Lever b Doshi	21	
G. B. Stevenson not out	27	
D. L. Underwood b Ghavri	1	
B 8, l-b 9, n-b 14	31	B 3, l-b 1, n-b 2 6
	296	**(0 wkts) 98**

1/21 2/21 3/45 4/57 5/58
6/229 7/245 8/262 9/283

Bowling: *First Innings*—Dev 29–8–64–3; Ghavri 20.1–5–52–5; Binny 19–3–70–1; Doshi 23–6–57–1; Yadav 6–2–22–0. *Second Innings*—Dev 8–2–21–0; Ghavri 5–0–12–0; Patil 3–0–8–0; Yadav 6–0–31–0; Doshi 6–1–12–0; Gavaskar 1–0–4–0; Viswanath 0.3–0–4–0.

Umpires: Hanumantha Rao and J. D. Ghosh.

England won by ten wickets.

INDEX